© 2002 Buddha's Light Publishing

Published by Buddha's Light Publishing
3456 South Glenmark Drive,
Hacienda Heights, CA 91745, USA
Telephone: 626-923-5143 / 626-961-9697,
Fax: 626-923-5145 / 626-369-1944
E-Mail: itc@blia.org

Chinese by Venerable Master Hsing Yun,
Translated into English from the Chinese by Amy Lam,
Edited by Robin Stevens and Brenda Bolinger,
Cover designed by Mei-Chi Shih.

ISBN: 0-9715612-3-0
Library of Congress Control Number: 2001099614

The Awakening Life
生活中的覺醒

Dharma Words
by
Venerable Master Hsing Yun

星雲大師法語

Translated by Amy Lam

林郭婉霞翻譯

目 錄
Contents

生活中充滿苦樂、有無、順逆、窮通、得失、無
常、在起伏不定的生活裡，我們怎樣來適應呢？

*...Conditions in life are unpredictable, ever-changing, and
impermanent in nature. The presence of one event is often
matched by the absence of its parallel event...*

在生活中修行

修行，不一定要到寺院，也不一定要像老僧入定，其實在我們的生活裏，做人處事都應該要有修行，有修養。日常生活的修行包括：

第一，衣食住行的修行：

比方說：穿衣只要樸素、保暖就好；吃飯，只要吃飽就好；住，只要空氣流通、安靜就好；行，「你騎馬來我騎驢，看看眼前不如你；回頭一看推車漢，比上不足比下餘」。因此，在衣、食、住、行裏，只要滿足、配合我們的身分，就是修行。

Cultivation in Our Daily Lives

To develop and deepen our spiritual practice, it is not necessary to retreat to a temple or meditate in isolation. Although these methods are beneficial to practitioners, true cultivation occurs in the midst of our daily lives.

How do we practice cultivation in our daily lives?

1. Cultivate a proper attitude toward the four basic needs: clothing, food, housing, and transportation.

As the main purpose of clothing is to keep us warm and protect us from the elements, simple and plain clothing is sufficient. Food is essential to satisfy our hunger and maintain our health; a plain meal is adequate to fulfill this need. Regarding housing, plenty of fresh air and a quiet environment are sufficient. Concerning transportation, consider this saying: I ride a donkey behind your horse; compared to you, I have less. Behind me, a man pulls a cart; I do not have less anymore.

When our very basic needs are satisfied and we are content with our circumstances, this is true cultivation.

第二，身心活動的修行：

一個人每天手要做事，腳要走路，眼睛要看，耳朵要聽，心裏要想、要分別，所以在身心的活動裏，要做到手不打人，嘴不罵人，眼不亂看，所謂君子「十目所視，十手所指」，舉心動念都應該是合情、合理、合法的。

第三，人際關係的修行：

在人際關係裏如何修行？人我相處時，不要看不起人、嫉妒人、欺負人，應該尊重別人。抱持你大我小、你對我錯、你有我無、你樂我苦的觀念，這樣就能促進人際的關係。

2. Cultivate the activities of body and mind.

Everyone relies upon their hands to work, their feet to walk, their eyes to see, their ears to hear, and their minds to think. As our daily lives depend on these activities of the body and mind, each movement be it physical or mental should be guided by our practice. There are basic guidelines that need to be observed. Hands shall not be used for fighting; mouths shall not be used to criticize with malice; eyes shall not wander without purpose; all behaviors should be responsible and respectful. Concerning our mind, all thoughts should be grounded in wholesome subjects and in the spirit of goodwill.

3. Cultivate relationships with others.

How do we practice cultivation in our relationships with others? In our daily interactions, we should not look down upon people, be jealous, or take advantage of them. It is important to respect everyone without discrimination. Offer your kindness to others by cultivating the attitude that they deserve first priority and that you are content with second; they are right and you are wrong; they should have and you will not; they should enjoy pleasure and you will endure pain. Developing a selfless attitude in all matters will significantly improve one s relationships with others.

第四，金錢財物的修行：

自己不要太過自私、太過貪心，喜捨是很重要的，金錢不是一切。金錢可以是毒蛇，也可以是良藥，端看使用金錢者的心態。要會用錢，不要成為錢財的奴隸，才是財物之利。

4. Cultivate the wise use of money.

Regarding wealth, we should not be selfish or greedy. We should realize the importance of making offerings and feel pleased to do so, for money is not everything. Depending on the wisdom and cultivation of those who give and spend money, their intentions can be as poisonous as a snake or as helpful as medicine in times of illness. When we manage our money properly, we do not become its slave, and we can use it for beneficial purposes.

在生活中修行，有四點參考：

第一，衣食住行的修行。

第二，身心活動的修行。

第三，人際關係的修行。

第四，金錢財物的修行。

The four suggestions for cultivation in our daily lives are:

1. Cultivate a proper attitude toward the four basic needs: clothing, food, housing, and transportation.
2. Cultivate the activities of body and mind.
3. Cultivate relationships with others.
4. Cultivate the wise use of money.

怎樣生活

我們可曾反省日常的生活，是怎麼樣過的？生活要有計劃，諸如經濟、作息，甚至是在家中的一舉一動……等，都要有計劃。凡事一有了計劃，都會事半功倍。

生活中充滿苦樂、有無、順逆、窮通、得失、起伏無常，在起伏不定的生活裏，我們怎樣來適應呢？

第一，要隨遇而安：

在隨遇而安的生活裏，有也好，無也好，多也好，少也好，甚至光榮也好，侮辱也好，都不要太計較窮通得失、順利有無，遇到什麼都能接受，都能安住，就是隨遇而安！

How to Live

Have we ever reflected on how we conduct our everyday lives? It is essential to have some form of planning for our conduct. We need to plan ahead on household activities and other daily matters. These activities, properly planned, can be more effectively and efficiently completed.

Conditions in life are unpredictable, ever-changing, and impermanent in nature. The presence of one event is often matched by the absence of its parallel event; the opposite conditions of suffering and happiness, to have and have not, favorable and unfavorable circumstances, success and failure, and gain and loss are some examples. How should we conduct ourselves in handling the changing conditions in life?

1. Accept the reality of changing circumstances with an unperturbed and peaceful mind.

When there is a change in circumstance, we need to accept it with an unperturbed and peaceful mind, no matter what happens, whether we gain or lose something or receive honor or insult. We should not be too concerned about success or failure, gains or losses, favorable or unfavorable circumstances, and whether we have or have not.

第二，要隨緣生活：

在我們的生活中，或早或晚，或和好人相處，或與壞人為伍，或佔便宜，或吃悶虧。在這善與不善的因緣裏，我們要隨緣生活。

2. Adjust our living according to circumstances.

We often experience both good and bad situations in life. We might be associated with the good or bad company of others. We might take advantage of others or be betrayed by them. In all of these situations, whether good or bad, we need to adjust the conduct of our living according to the prevailing circumstances.

第三，要隨心自在：

我們的心在生活裏要感到自在，不起差別愛憎的念頭，就像觀音菩薩叫觀自在。觀人自在，是說我的心看人很自在；觀事自在，我看一切事很自在；觀境自在，我對一切境界都很自在。所以，我們的心能夠安住在自在中。

3. Cultivate a mind that is free from worry and delusion.

Emulating the Avalokitesvara Bodhisattva we need to cultivate and attain a mind that is free from all worries and delusions, a non-discriminating mind that does not make any distinction between desire or love and dislike or hate. With such a mind we will be able to treat all people without prejudice, look at all phenomena with insight and clarity, and view all spheres of perception without delusion.

第四，要隨喜而作：

不要苦苦惱惱，心不甘情不願的工作，應抱著充滿歡喜、樂趣

4. Carry out our duties and responsibilities with joy.

We should not carry out our duties and responsibilities with

understanding among people. What is more important is our ability to put this knowledge into practice. For instance, we may talk about the four infinite states of mind: limitless loving-kindness (maitri), limitless compassion (karuna), limitless joy (mudita), and limitless equanimity (upeksa). Are we able to put these four virtues into practice in our relationships with all kinds of people? Are we able to control our hatred and anger when we are in a rage?

第三，重於隨緣也要重於不變：

在佛教裏常聽到兩句話：「不變隨緣，隨緣不變」，重視隨緣的生活才能隨時自在，不會有過份希求的痛苦，但也要重視不變的生活，才能不變原則，不產生波動不已的恐懼感。

3. Hold fast to the basic principles of right living and adjust according to ever-changing circumstances.

In Buddhism, we often come across the following two common verses: Though every phenomenon arises according to changing circumstances, its true nature remains unchanged," and "Though each phenomenon has an invariant true nature, the form of its arising varies with changing circumstances, free of all worries and obstructions at all times and not subject to the suffering of excessive desire."

One who holds fast to right living is unlikely to change the basic principle of his or her conduct, and therefore will not be troubled by the perpetual and unsettling feelings of fear that arise in daily life.

第四，重於世樂也要重於法樂：

信佛學佛，不是為了受苦而來的；信佛學佛，是為了追尋快樂而來的。因此，我們追求世間的快樂，諸如養花蒔草、旅遊娛樂的世樂，但更要有增長見識、聽聞佛法的法樂。世樂是一時的、短暫的，而法樂是追求真理的快樂、祥悅的快樂，是永恒的、長久的。

4. Pursue Dharma joy in addition to worldly pleasures.

Embracing and practicing Buddhism does not stem from the need to endure suffering but rather from the motivation to seek happiness. Therefore, in addition to pursuing worldly pleasures such as those derived from gardening, vacations, and amusement, more importantly we should pursue Dharma joy by broadening our horizons and learning and practicing the Buddha's teachings. Worldly pleasures are temporary and short-lived in nature. On the other hand, Dharma joy is the result of pursuing the truth. It is the joy of peace and harmony, and is permanent and everlasting in nature.

我們每日生活的態度是：

第一，重於物質也要重於精神。

第二，重於言說也要重於修行。

第三，重於隨緣也要重於不變。

第四，重於世樂也要重於法樂。

Our attitude toward life is therefore fourfold:

1. Pursue spiritual needs in addition to material desires.
2. Engage in cultivation in addition to pursuing knowledge acquired in words.
3. Hold fast to the basic principles of right living and adjust according to ever-changing circumstances.
4. Pursue Dharma joy in addition to worldly pleasures.

如何過一日生活

禪宗說：「日日是好日」，我們要把每一天過得很實在，今天把今天過好，一月把一月過好，才會一年一年的過好；一年一年的過好，才會一生的過好，我們如何過一日的生活？我有四點意見：

第一，每日說好話：

一天當中，你自己盤算一下，你說了多少的好話？過去袁了凡先生，他每天都用「功過格」檢討自己的功過，反省一天之中有多少功德過失，並且老實做記錄。比方說：我們每天跟人家講話：「你早！你好！」就是好話；「謝謝你、對不起」，這就是好話；「我有什麼能為你服務嗎？我想為你盡一點心力」，這都是好話；或者你見到一位太太，讚美她的家，讚美她的兒女，讚美她的丈夫；你見到一個學生，你讚美他的老師，讚美他的學校；你見到一個公務員，你讚美他的同事，他的長官，你能每日多說好話，就有個美好的一日。

examine ourselves frequently, can transform wrongful behavior o goodness.

Be more joyful everyday.

If we are constantly worried and this l, this misery will show on our so mes and each day will be difficult. wever, if we can have pleasant lings and live more joyfully ile eating, sleeping, or visiting ers, we will enjoy each moment life. When we live each day with re joy, we can easily have a plea- t day.

Therefore, the four suggestions out how to live each day are:

Speak thoughtful words every- day.

Perform thoughtful deeds every- day.

Practice self-examination every- day.

Be more joyful everyday.

接心

古人說：「人之相交，貴在知心」。想要結交一個知心的朋友並不容易，因此可見知音的可貴。在修道的途中，非常講究師徒之間的接心，老師和學生之間思想要能交流，在思想、見解上可以得到老師的真傳，這就叫做接心。所以，我們不管交朋友也好，受教也好，接心很重要。如何和父母、師長、朋友接心呢？

第一，見解一致：

見解一致，大家才能同一步伐，才能同心協力，並駕齊驅。

The Connection between Hearts and Minds

There is an old Chinese saying that goes like this: What makes friendship valuable is the connection between hearts and minds. Based on the fact that it is not easy to have friends who can read your heart and mind, we know how precious this can be. On the path of cultivation, the connection of hearts and minds between masters and students is very important. It is only when masters and students can communicate their thoughts and ideas that the knowledge of masters can be transferred to students. This is what is meant by the phrase connection between hearts and minds. Thus, regardless of whether you are making friends or obtaining an education, the connection between hearts and minds is very important. How do we go about connecting our hearts and minds with our parents, teachers, and friends?

1. Establish common understanding.

When we have common understanding, we can walk through life in unison. We can work toward the same goal and make progress together.

第二，思想統一：

很多問題的產生，都是由於思想不統一所致，所以思想統一很重要。

第三，精神相依：

既然相知、相遇，精神上更要互相依靠。

第四，甘苦與共：

就是同甘共苦、患難與共的意思。

第五，生死不易：

面臨生死的時候，不以存亡易心。

第六，榮辱不離：

光榮、侮辱互相分享，互相分擔，永遠不離開。

2. Establish common ground in ways of thinking.

Many problems arise when we are divergent in our ways of thinking. It is very important to establish common ground in our ways of thinking.

3. Rely on each other in spirit.

As long as two people have the opportunity to meet and become friends, they should also rely on each other in spirit.

4. Share both joy and sorrow.

We should be able to share the comforts and hardships in our lives. During hard times, we should support and encourage each other.

5. Remain loyal to each other even in the face of death.

Even when we are confronted with life and death decisions, we should not betray our friends for our own benefit or gain. We should remain loyal to each other.

6. Go through times of honor and disgrace together.

We should share the joys of glory as well as shoulder the burdens of disgrace. We should commit to each other forever.

第七，兩心相通：

　兩個人相處，要培養默契，才能心心相印。

第八，人我一如：

　你也好，我也好，你我是一體的，能夠泯滅彼此的對待，就能人我一如，彼此同心。

所以，不管交朋友，或和老師接心，應該：

第一，　見解一致。

第二，　思想統一。

第三，　精神相依。

第四，　甘苦與共。

第五，　生死不易。

第六，　榮辱不離。

第七，　兩心相通。

第八，　人我一如。

7. Develop tacit understanding.

When we interact with our friends, we will gradually develop tacit understanding with them. This way our friendships will be strengthened.

8. Make no distinctions between self and other.

We should try to treat others as we would ourselves, as if they are not separate from us. If we eradicate the duality of self and other, there is no distinction between ourselves and our friends. In this way, we can be united in heart and mind.

Regardless of whether we are making friends or connecting our hearts and minds with our teachers, we should:

1. Establish common understanding.
2. Establish common ground in our ways of thinking.
3. Rely on each other in spirit.
4. Share both joy and sorrow.
5. Remain loyal to each other even in the face of death.
6. Go through times of honor and disgrace together.
7. Develop tacit understanding.
8. Make no distinctions between self and other.

養心

我們經常勸別人要保重身體，卻很少想到要保養心理。實際上養心比養身更重要，因為心理的建設、心理的健全，能增加身體的健康，所以如何養心呢？我有四點意見：

第一，以和平願力來養心：

我們的心裏，要有和平的觀念，要有悲心願力。因為我們的心就像工廠，你有和平、願力，自能用和平的心，用願力的心去造福別人。

第二，以般若福慧來養心：

如果我們的心裏沒有般若智慧，沒有福德善念，就像一個工廠沒有資源，沒有原料，就不能出產好的產品。假如我們的心中充滿「般若的泉水」、「智慧的泉水」，就能涓涓不斷的流出智慧和福報。

第三，以菩提禪淨來養心：

人有時候有妄想，有煩惱，有是非，有差別，所以要有菩提正

Nurture the Mind

We often advise others to take care of their health, but we seldom think of nurturing the mind. Actually, nurturing the mind is much more important than taking care of our health. Our mental health can improve our physical health. How do we nurture our mind? I have four suggestions to offer:

1. Use equanimity and willpower to nurture the mind.

We should be mindful of equanimity, compassion, and willpower. The mind is like a factory. If we are equanimous and determined, we will be able to do a lot of good for others.

2. Use prajna, or wisdom, to nurture the mind.

Without prajna, or wisdom, one is like a factory without raw materials, which undoubtedly would fail to produce any fine products. On the contrary, if one s mind is filled with the spring water of prajna, then one will always exude wisdom and blessings will follow.

3. Use meditative concentration and purity to nurture the mind.

Our minds often become agitated

覺，要用禪定來養心，要用念佛的清淨心來養心。就如一缸渾濁的水，把明礬放進去就清淨了。對於我們妄念雜染的心，要用正念去清淨，用菩提去清淨，用念佛去清淨，我們的心自然就清淨了。

第四，以空無包容來養心：

有時候我們的心量狹小，不能容物，假如心胸像虛空宇宙，就能包容世界萬有。所謂「宰相肚裏能撐船」，我們要能容納異己的存在，這樣心胸才會寬廣。

with high hopes, worry, judgements, and discriminations. We can purify the mind with right understanding, meditative concentration, and serenity by reciting the Buddha s name. A jug of dirty, disturbed water can become clean and settled if we put alum into it. To purify our mind, we should use right thoughts, understanding, and recite the Buddha s name. In this way, our minds will become cleansed.

4. Use emptiness and tolerance to nurture the mind.

Sometimes the scope of our minds is too small to accommodate anything. If our minds can be expansive like the boundless universe, we then could accommodate the world. There is an old Chinese saying that describes how tolerant we can be even in high positions: One can row a boat within the belly of the chief minister. It is only when we can accept those who are different from us that our minds can grow.

所以如何養心？

第一，以和平願力來養心。

第二，以般若福慧來養心。

第三，以菩提禪淨來養心。

第四，以空無包容來養心。

How do we nurture the mind?

1. Use equanimity and willpower to nurture the mind.
2. Use prajna, or wisdom, to nurture the mind.
3. Use meditative concentration and purity to nurture the mind.
4. Use emptiness and tolerance to nurture the mind.

擒山中之賊易，擒心中之賊難。

...It is easy to arrest the bandits of the mountains,
but hard to capture thieves of the mind...

治心

Take Charge of the Mind

俗語說：「治國容易，治家難」。歷史上有名的將相可以把國家治理得很好，可是回到家裏，有時候連妻子、兒女都沒有辦法對治。

有的人治家很好，治心很難，他把家庭管理得很好，可是自己內心的貪、瞋、愚痴、邪念等等，卻沒有辦法，常常為了心裏的七情六慾而苦惱。所以，治心也是人生的一大課題。

如何治心呢？我有四點建議：

第一，要懂得收心：

我們的心像猴子，又像盜賊，我們不可以任它在外面為非作歹。王陽明先生說得很好：「擒山中之賊易，擒心中之賊難」。山寨裏的土匪強盜容易抓，心裏的土匪強盜很難抓。佛教說：「所謂一切法，為治一切心；若無一

There is an old saying, It is easy to manage a country, but it s difficult to manage one s family. During the course of history, there were many famous generals and ministers who were very capable in managing their countries but failed miserably in their relationships with their wives and children.

There have also been many people who took good care of their families but failed to take charge of their minds. Those people are at a loss for how to deal with their greed, hatred, ignorance, and false beliefs. They become enslaved to the emotions and desires of the mind. Thus, it is very important to know how to take charge of the mind.

How do we take charge of the mind? I have four suggestions:

1. Know how to control the mind.

Our minds are active, like monkeys or thieves; we cannot let our minds run wild and loose. It was said that, It is easy to arrest the bandits of the mountains, but hard to capture thieves of the mind. There is a common saying in Buddhism

切心，何須一切法？」所以我們要懂得收心，要有方法來收攝我們的心，不要讓它亂跑。

that, All dharmas exist to heal all troubles of the mind. If there were not so many delusions of the mind, why would we need all these dharmas? We have to know how to control our minds and not to go astray.

第二，要懂得修心：

桌子壞了，把它修理一下就可以用了；衣服壞了，把它縫補一下也可以再穿；房子漏水，修理一下就不會再漏水了。我們的心壞了，心中充滿貪欲、瞋恨、愚痴、驕傲、我慢，也應該把它修理一下。

2. Know how to cultivate the mind.

When a desk is broken, it can only be used once it is repaired. When clothing is ripped, it can only be worn once it is mended. When a roof leaks, the problem is fixed only once it is patched. When our minds are corrupted, they are filled with greed, hatred, ignorance, vanity, and arrogance. We need to mend our minds as well.

第三，要懂得用心：

有的人常常被心所用，自己不會用心。所謂心為形役，我們的心常被五欲六塵左右，被外境的色、聲、香、味、觸、法所左右，因而引起貪念及憎恨，所以我們要懂得用心，才不會起無明。

3. Know how to apply the mind.

Some people become slaves to their minds; they do not know how to apply their minds. We can become distracted by the desires of wealth, sex, fame, food, and sleep. When our minds are easily influenced by the external stimuli of form, sound, smell, touch, and perception, greed and hatred will often follow. Thus, we have to know how to apply our minds and not become deluded.

第四，要懂得明心：

禪宗講「明心見性」，就是要明白自己的心，要清楚當下的每一刻，這樣才能夠明心見性，凡事也就容易成功了。

所以，治心之道是：

第一，要懂得收心。

第二，要懂得修心。

第三，要懂得用心。

第四，要懂得明心。

4. Know how to understand the mind.

The Chan school of Buddhism urges all of us to understand our minds and see our true nature. When we can understand our minds every moment, then we can see our true nature and success will come easily.

Thus, the ways to take charge of our minds are:

1. Know how to control the mind.
2. Know how to cultivate the mind.
3. Know how to apply the mind.
4. Know how to understand the mind.

去除心病

我們的身體常常有頭痛、肚子痛、胃痛等毛病，我們的心理也有毛病，心理上的毛病就是貪、瞋、痴、慢、疑。如何去除心理上的毛病呢？我有四句偈給各位參考：

We often come down with physical ailments such as headaches and stomachaches. Our minds can get weak, too. Sicknesses of the mind include greed, hatred, ignorance, arrogance, and suspicion. How do we rid ourselves of the sicknesses of the mind? I would like to offer four suggestions:

第一，要求不著急：

貪念之心，人人皆有！但是我們要能夠控制自己的貪心，不能貪求無厭，心中有所要求也不著急馬上實現。比方過去我有個心願，希望成立一個圖書館，於是我就慢慢地買書，十年、二十年、三十年，只要我持續的買下去，必定能夠成立一個圖書館。現在我已經建立好多個圖書館了。我想要成立一個佛教博物館，我就慢慢地搜集佛教文物，我相信只要我不死，十年、二十年、三十年，總有一天會完成願望，現在佛光山已經有一個佛教文物陳列館了，所以「要求不著急」。時下的年輕人就是貪心，太著急，希望立刻擁有一切，於是自己製造心理上的毛病。

1. Do not be impatient in pursuing goals.

We all have desires and wishes. The important thing is to be able to control our greed and not fall into the trap of always wanting more. When we desire something, we should not be impatient and hasty in reaching our goals. For example, I wanted to set up a library. With this goal in mind, I started a book collection. I was convinced that if I did not give up, one day, be it in ten, twenty, or thirty years, I would realize my goal. Now, I have established a few libraries.

I also wanted to set up a Buddhist museum. Slowly I collected various kinds of Buddhist artwork. I believed that my goal would materialize one day as long as I persevered and did not give up. Today, Fo Guang Shan has its own museum of Buddhist artwork. Thus, it is important that we are not hasty or impatient about reaching our goals. Greed affects many young people today; they are impatient and wish to own everything instantly. In so doing, their minds become sick.

第二，脾氣慢半拍：

我們發脾氣的時候，只要肯對自己說：等一會兒，慢五分鐘，我想一想。如此脾氣就發不起來了，憎恨心就消除了。

2. Slow down when you are about to lose your temper.

When we are about to lose our temper, we should say to ourselves, Pause, take five deep breaths, and think it over. This will give our minds a chance to calm down, and our tempers will not flare up. In this way, anger and hatred will vanish.

第三，痴迷轉靈巧：

我們愚痴、迷惑、不明理都是由於固執己見，假如我們能夠多為對方著想，凡事合於公道，如此，就能夠轉愚痴為靈巧了。

3. Turn ignorance around.

We are ignorant, deluded, and unreasonable when we cling to our own points of view. If we can put others first and act fairly, then we can turn our ignorance around.

第四，疑嫉化祥和：

人和人相處，經常會有疑心、嫉妒心。常常別人在講話，本來與我無關，可是以為他們一定是在批評我，看到一點風，就聯想到一陣雨，所以在心中產生狐疑，有了狐疑，就無法信賴別人，對國家社會、對親朋好友、對宗教信仰也就不能生起信心。

4. Transform jealousy and suspicion into peace and harmony.

In our dealings with others, it is easy to become jealous and suspicious. When others gossip, we may become suspicious and think that they are criticizing us. It is just like the saying, When we feel a light breeze, we start to imagine an immense storm.

If we are suspicious, we will not

trust anyone. We eventually will lose faith in our country, society, family, and good friends. Even our religious faith will suffer and will have no chance to sprout and grow.

所以，如何去除貪、瞋、痴、慢、疑？應該牢記以下四點：

第一，要求不著急。

第二，脾氣慢半拍。

第三，痴迷轉靈巧。

第四，疑嫉化祥和。

How do we rid ourselves of greed, hatred, ignorance, arrogance, and suspicion? We should remember the following four points:

1. Do not be impatient in pursuing goals.
2. Slow down when you are about to lose your temper.
3. Turn ignorance around.
4. Transform jealousy and suspicion into peace and harmony.

心理的病態 (一)

每個人都有生病的時候，身體有病，就要給醫生看。我們的心理也會害病，心理的病，就是貪婪、瞋恨、愚痴、嫉妒、邪見……等等。心理上有病時，也應該設法加以治療，身體骯髒時要用水來洗，心理上有了骯髒，則要用真理的法水來洗淨。

心理上到底有些什麼病？什麼是心理的病態呢？

第一，幸災樂禍：

有的人，看到人家富有、成功，就嫉妒他；看到人家受苦受難，反而很得意，甚至落井下石，這種幸災樂禍的心理就是病態。

第二，同歸於盡：

一般人都不希望別人好，譬如看到這個人很會做學問，就說做學問有什麼好；看到人家事業有成，又說會做事業有什麼了不起。總要說些冷言冷語，總希望

Symptoms of a Sick Mind (I)

We all get sick once in a while. When we are sick, we need to go to the doctor. Our minds can also become ill. Sicknesses of the mind include greed, hatred, ignorance, jealousy, etc. When our minds are ill, we should also seek treatment so that our minds can get well. We bathe when our bodies are filthy; similarly, when our mind is defiled, we need to cleanse it with the water of the Dharma.

What are some sicknesses of the mind? And what are the symptoms?

1. Taking pleasure in others misfortune.

Some people envy others who are rich and successful, they also take pleasure in seeing others suffer. They may even strike when others are down. Taking pleasure in others misfortune is a symptom of a sick mind.

2. Wishing to bring others down with you.

Many people who have failed do not want to see others excel. When they meet with the learned, they put down the value of knowledge. When they see someone

別人這個不好，那個不好，最後世間上的所有人都不好，這就是「同歸於盡」的心理病態

succeed, they make light of their success. These people are sarcastic and enjoy putting others down. They hope to see others fail. Wishing to drag others down with you is another symptom of a sick mind.

第三，磨人為樂：

青年守則裡有一則「助人為快樂之本」，但現在社會上卻出現一個現象，以折磨別人為快樂。尤其是官僚主義盛行，有事請這種人幫忙，他便推三阻四的折磨你，這就是「磨人為快樂之本」的心理病態。

3. Finding joy in irritating others.

There are also people who find joy in irritating others. When someone asks them for help, they find joy in irritating the person and giving him or her the run-around. Finding joy in irritating others is another symptom of a sick mind.

第四，損人為己：

一般人都有私心，所以經常為了一己之利而侵損別人，這就是損人為己。另有一種人，甚至做出損人不利己的事，這是一種嚴重的心理病態。

如果我們能將這些心理病態治療好，必能改善我們不易團結的缺點。

人的**心理病態是**：

第一，幸災樂禍。

第二，同歸於盡。

第三，磨人為樂。

第四，損人為己。

4.　Benefiting one s self at the expense of others.

Most of us tend to think only about ourselves and frequently end up trying to benefit ourselves at the expense of others, while some may even harm others without even benefiting themselves. This is a symptom of a seriously sick mind.

If we can heal ourselves, we can enhance the cohesiveness of all people.

Symptoms of a sick mind are:

1. Taking pleasure in others misfortune.
2. Wishing to drag others down with you.
3. Finding joy in irritating others.
4. Benefiting one s self at the expense of others.

心理的病態（二）

人的心理病態除了上述的四點之外，我再舉出四種：

In addition to the four symptoms of a sick mind addressed in the previous section, I will list four additional symptoms:

第一，損人不利己的心理病態：

有些人做事，從不考慮清楚，對他人有利的事情他不做，甚至對他人有害，對自己也有害的事，他卻糊里糊塗地做，因而造成損人又不利己的後果，自己也有虧道德、操守。

1. Harming others and not benefiting one s self.

Some people never think before they act. They do not do anything that benefits others. Clouded and confused, their actions cause harm to others as well as to themselves. As a result, they end up harming others and not benefiting themselves. Additionally, their personal integrity and moral standards are compromised.

第二，信壞不信好的心理病態：

所謂「好事不出門，壞事傳千里」，有的人，你跟他介紹一個好人、說一件好事，他不相信。但說那個人偷竊，那個人強盜，那個人家有姦情，他就信以為真，這就是信壞不信好的心理病態。

2. Believing in bad things instead of good things.

Just like the saying, Good news does not travel, bad news travels wide, there are some people who refuse to believe you when you introduce them to a nice person or tell them good news. On the other hand, they accept without question when told that a person is a thief or a rapist. This is the syndrome of believing in the bad instead of the good.

第三，畏果不畏因的心理病態：

有些人做壞事的時候，心中總是抱著僥倖的心理，等到果報來了，才開始後悔，才感到驚慌畏懼，這就是畏果不畏因的心理病態。

第四，信假不信眞的心理病態：

一般人都喜歡聽好聽的話，乃至褒獎自己的話，因此眞話他不相信，寧可相信假話，這是人的劣根性。

以上這些心理的病態如果不除，好的善法便不能灌注到自己的身心裡，反而讓世間上的罪惡、虛偽常駐心中，造成病態心理。因此，我們應該經常自我觀照，自我療病。

3. Fearing effects instead of causes.

When some people commit trespasses, they hope that they can escape the wheels of justice. It is only when the effects of their bad causes are ripened that they begin to feel remorseful and frightened. This is the syndrome of fearing effects instead of causes.

4. Believing in falsehoods rather than the truth.

Most people prefer pleasantries, even flatteries, to the truth. They would rather believe in falsehoods. This is a deep-rooted weakness of human nature. If we cannot rid ourselves of our morbidity, not only will the good and virtuous Dharma be unable to reach into our bodies and minds, the evilness and vanity of this world will forever live in our minds, which will in turn become morbid. We should constantly reflect upon and examine ourselves and heal ourselves of our own sicknesses.

人的心理病態是：

第一，損人不利己的心理病態。

第二，信壞不信好的心理病態。

第三，畏果不畏因的心理病態。

第四，信假不信真的心理病態。

Symptoms of a sick mind include:

1. Harming others and not benefiting one s self.
2. Believing in bad things instead of good things.
3. Fearing effects instead of causes.
4. Believing in falsehoods rather than the truth.

障道的因缘

障道的因緣，就是我們做事情常常遇到障礙。讀書遇到障礙了，交朋友遇到障礙了，留學遇到障礙了，創辦事業遇到障礙了，甚至於要建一棟房子，要買一個像具都遇到障礙了，連修行、信仰也遇到障礙了。障道的因緣在哪裡呢？有四點：

第一，口說不行：

真正障礙我們的還是我們自己。外來的障礙力量有限，自我障礙的力量很強大。口說不行，常常說，說了又不做，說久了以後人家不相信你，這時候就是障道了。

第二，心想諂曲：

你心裡所想的，都是打別人的主意，都是自私，都是自己多得到一點利益。這種諂曲不正的心，別人不是盲目的，也不是糊塗的。他會知道，他不但看到你

The Causes and Conditions of Our Misfortune

Life is full of obstacles and misfortune. Sometimes, we have trouble making friends, and other times we have trouble in our studies. Some people have a bumpy career, while others have a tough time finding the right house for their family. Obstacles can arise in whatever we do, even in our religious practice. What are the causes and conditions of our misfortune? There are four causes I would like to discuss.

1. Not keeping promises.

We are our own worst enemy. In most cases, external factors are secondary compared to the troubles we bring upon ourselves. Take the example of not keeping our promises. When others find out that we do not keep our promises, they will not trust us anymore. In this way, we are making our lives miserable.

2. Harboring ill thoughts.

If we are always scheming to take advantage of others, very soon others will see through our selfishness. People are not stupid, and our facade will soon become transparent. Others will realize our

的人，看到你的面孔，也看到你的心，你的心諂曲，他當然不要和你來往。

ulterior motives and distance themselves from us.

第三，身行惡事：

你如果生活中有很多不良記錄，交朋友沒有信用，自私、見利忘義，甚至做過很多非法的事情，當然別人就不願跟你合作，不跟你來往，所以身行惡事也是障道的因緣。

3. Behaving badly.

If we have a history of bad conduct in our lives, such as disloyalty to our friends, selfish behavior, ungratefulness, or acting unethically, it is only natural that others would refuse to have anything to do with us. Therefore, if we do not mind our actions, we can become the cause of our own downfall.

第四，人我計較：

你和人相處，和人合作，和人創業，不要錙銖必較。你計較很多，人家當然不願跟你建立太密切的關係，很多好因緣往往是自己把它破壞了。我們如果不改正自己的因緣，就永遠有障礙。

4. Being overly exacting.

If we are overly exacting in the way we deal with others, we may put others off. They may think twice before they have anything to do with us. In this way, we are destroying for ourselves whatever opportunities there are. If we do not change our ways, we are creating the causes and conditions of our own future misfortune.

所以障礙我們因緣的是：

第一，口說不行。

第二，心想諂曲。

第三，身行惡事。

第四，人我計較。

What are the causes and conditions of our own misfortune? They are:

1. Not keeping promises.
2. Harboring ill thoughts.
3. Behaving badly.
4. Being overly exacting.

佛教對神通的看法

現代人常好奇的想學神通，神通雖然有，但最好不要學，更不能有神通，因為一般人有神通是不利於己的。例如：我現在沒有他心通，你批評我、怨恨我，我不知道，我仍然對你很好。相反地，我有了他心通後，知道你心裡對我很不滿意，我的日子也不好過。

又如，我明天會死，因為我不知道，所以今天我活得很快樂；現在有了宿命通，預知二十年後會死，三十年後會死，就活得很不安心。所以有了神通，不一定很好，重要的是我們對神通應該要有正確的認識：

第一，神通非究竟之法：

神通不是了脫生死的究竟之法，它不但不能增進道德，脫離苦惱，不慎使用，有時反而成為

The Buddhist Perspective on Supernatural Power

Many people are often intrigued by the manifestation of supernatural power. Supernatural power does indeed exist, but it is best not to pursue or possess it. For most of us, the possession of supernatural power can do us more harm than good. Let me give you some examples. I do not have the ability to read the minds of others. Since I am not privy to any criticisms or dislikes others may harbor in their minds about me, we remain on good terms with each other. On the other hand, if I can read the inner thoughts of others, I may feel compelled to react to them and thus jeopardize my relationships.

I also cannot foretell the future. So if I were to pass away tomorrow, I still have peace of mind today. The possession of supernatural power is not necessarily desirable. It is more important to have the right understanding of what supernatural power means.

1. Supernatural power is not the ultimate practice in life.

Supernatural power cannot help us to become better people, and it definitely cannot free us from the

進趨解脫之道的障礙，俗話說：「淹死會水的，打死會拳的。」不要以為神通是萬能的，有了神通就可以萬事無恐。

第二，神通敵不過業力：

在世間上，最大的力量不是神通，而是行為的力量，也就是業的力量。你縱有再大的神通，可是終究敵不過業力，如神通第一的目犍連，就遭到被外道殺害的業報。所以，業報來的時候，神通也沒用。

cycle of rebirth. When one possesses supernatural power, it does not necessarily mean one is exempt from problems in life. If not used with caution, supernatural power can actually become an obstacle in our practice. There is an ancient Chinese saying, Those who can swim, drown; those who can fight, die. This is similar to a common saying in English that a little knowledge is a dangerous thing. We should not be lured into thinking that supernatural power is the be all and end all.

2. Supernatural power cannot nullify the force of karma.

The most powerful force in this world is not supernatural power but the force of karma. Karma is a Sanskrit word which means action or deed. We all have to live with the consequences of our actions. Regardless of how great our supernatural power is we still cannot evade the force of karma. Among the Buddha s disciples, Maudgalyayana was foremost in supernatural power. However, he was unable to escape the retribution of his unwholesome karma and died a violent death. When our time for retribution comes, even supernatural power cannot shield us from it.

第三，神通比不上道德：

初學佛法的人往往對一些神奇怪異的事情，興趣特別濃厚，而忽略了更重要的道德修養，其實智慧的顯發要透過甚深的禪定工夫，而禪定工夫的培養，有賴平日持戒的嚴謹，因此學佛應該從道德、慈悲入門。

第四，神通及不上空無：

神通是應有形有相上求，而般若的空理無所不遍，無所不在，只要在生活中擁有般若智慧，懂得空諸所有，可以放下一切，可以無我不計較、不執著，終生受用不盡。

3. Supernatural power does not supercede morality.

Beginners of Buddhism are often awed by the manifestation of supernatural power and may end up neglecting the important practice of developing their character and observing the percepts.

4. Supernatural power cannot compare to emptiness.

The display of supernatural power is still very much confined to the realm of the physical world. On the other hand, emptiness pervades everything. When we have insight into emptiness, we will be able to see that emptiness is the basis of existence and that there is no need for us to cling to anything in particular. We will be able to expand our horizons and be more accommodating of others. The understanding of emptiness is much more beneficial to us and can carry us through the ups and downs of life.

因此，佛教對神通的看法有四點：

第一，神通非究竟之法。

第二，神通敵不過業力。

第三，神通比不上道德。

第四，神通及不上空無。

In conclusion, the Buddhist views on supernatural power are:

1. Supernatural power is not the ultimate practice in life.
2. Supernatural power cannot nullify the force of karma.
3. Supernatural power does not supercede morality.
4. Supernatural power cannot compare to emptiness.

追求開悟證果是一般人學佛的最高目標!
「悟」是什麼? 悟了以後又是什麼樣的境界?

*...Many Buddhists aspire to attaining enlightenment
and achieving Buddhahood. What exactly does
enlightenment mean? How does it change a person?*

悟是什麼

追求開悟證果是一般人學佛的最高目標！「悟」是什麼？悟了以後又是什麼樣的境界？悟的那一刻，整個迷妄的世界都粉碎了，呈現在我們眼前的是另一種世界，另一種風光；悟的時候，久遠過去的事情會重新浮現在眼前；悟的時候，遙遠以前的人和事，也都會慢慢的向我們集中近來；悟的境界很難說，所謂「如人飲水，冷暖自知」，悟的那一刻，忽然沒有時間了，也沒有空間了。一切都是當然如是，本來如是。所以修道者追求「悟」，是一種無上的體會。那麼，悟是什麼呢？

第一，親證的體會：

吃飯，別人不能代我們吃飽；睡覺，別人也不能代我安睡，這完全是自我親身的證悟，一切的好和不好，在我內心有另外一種很強烈的感受。悟，就是親證的體會。

Enlightenment

Many Buddhists aspire to attaining enlightenment and achieving Buddhahood. What exactly does enlightenment mean? How does it change a person? It is said in the sutras that enlightenment is attained when delusion is replaced with clarity. One gains a new perspective on the world. Upon enlightenment, people and events from the distant past reappear in the mind. People and happenings from afar converge before us. It is difficult to describe the state of enlightenment and any portrayal can hardly do it justice. In enlightenment, the limitations of time and space do not exist. All things exist as they are and as they should be. Difficult as it may be, I will try to give my readers a basic description of what enlightenment is.

1. Enlightenment is understanding truth through experience.

There are certain things in life we have to do for ourselves. In our everyday living, no one can eat or sleep for us. In a similar way, no one can experience the truth for us; we have to experience it ourselves.

第二，透視的能力：

我們平常看世間，看人生，都是很浮面的，所謂「知其然，不知其所以然」，都只是在浮面上打轉，不能深透到裏面。「悟」了以後，看東西不再是光看表面，比方說：一張桌子，噢！桌子不是桌子，桌子是由木材做成；木材是由大樹長成；大樹則是由一粒種子，同時集合了陽光、空氣、水份等因緣而形成，所以從一張桌子，可以看到全宇宙的三千大千世界，這就是透視的能力。

第三，自我的覺醒：

「悟」，是自己「啊！我明白了，生從何來，死往何去？」「父母未生我之前，什麼是我本來面目？啊！我懂了！」這就是自我的覺醒。

2. Enlightenment is seeing through reality.

When we observe the world around us, our understanding of what is happening is quite superficial. Very often, we see things as they are, but we do not know why they are what they are. In other words, we have a very superficial understanding of reality. Enlightenment is the unveiled and profound seeing of the many aspects and layers of reality. When we look at a table, we see a flat surface supported by four legs. An enlightened individual sees that a table is not only made from wood, he or she sees that the wood for the table comes from trees. And a tree is the coming together of a seed, sunlight, air, moisture, and other numerous causes and conditions. From something as mundane as a table, we are able to see and understand all phenomena in the three thousand great chiliocosms. This is the power of penetrating vision.

3. Enlightenment is a state of self-awakening.

Enlightenment is when we say, Ah! I understand where life comes from and where death leads to. In the Chan school, enlightenment is characterized by the understanding of age-old questions such as, What was my original face before I was born?

第四，明白的領悟：

無論看人、看事，乃至於一切色、聲、香、味、觸等塵緣幻境，都能清清楚楚的領會，這就是明白的領悟。

所以悟的境界就是：

第一，親證的體會。

第二，透視的能力。

第三，自我的覺醒。

第四，明白的領悟。

4. Enlightenment is complete comprehension of all phenomena.

Why do we prefer some things instead of others? Why are we drawn to some people in particular? When we are able to fully understand all worldly phenomena, be it human relations, events, or our senses of sight, sound, smell, taste, and touch, we have complete comprehension.

In summary, enlightenment can be described as follows:

1. Enlightenment is understanding truth through experience.
2. Enlightenment is seeing through reality.
3. Enlightenment is a state of self-awakening.
4. Enlightenment is complete comprehension of all phenomena.

自悟修行

我們對於世上的知識、財富、愛情……等等，總是期望別人能教導我們、成全我們、愛護我們，甚至於覺悟成佛都希望別人幫忙。但就禪宗而言，世間上的一切事情，求人不如求己，凡事靠自己才是根本可行之道。

過去，有人問禪師：「怎樣才能開悟？」禪師回答：「我現在沒有時間說明，我要去吃飯了。」你能代他去吃飯嗎？他能代替你開悟嗎？吃飯、開悟，全在於自己。

如何自悟修行呢？也有四點：

第一，要自我觀照，反求諸己：
觀照自己在不在？觀照自己的心動不動？觀照自己能否把持自己？凡事要多多反求諸己，寬以待人。

The Road to Enlightenment is a Solitary One

When it comes to acquiring knowledge, accumulating wealth, or finding love, we often look to others for help. Sometimes, we even hope that others will simply do the job for us. The road to enlightenment, however, is one that we must travel ourselves. In the Chan school of Buddhism, there are many examples of teaching that speak to this point. Once a man asked a Chan master, Can you please show me the way to enlightenment? The Chan master replied, I do not have the time. I have to go and eat my lunch. Even a simple act like eating is something we have to do ourselves; no one can eat for us. Likewise, achieving enlightenment is a process upon which we must depend on ourselves.

What can we do to further our enlightenment? There are four points:

1. Use introspection and demand more of ourselves.

We can reflect on the presence of mind. Is our mind focused or wandering? Is our mind easily agitated? Are we in control of our mind? In all cases, we should continuously demand more of ourselves and be forgiving of others.

第二，要自我更新，不斷淨化：

自己的心要不斷的更新，不斷的淨化。我們的煩惱雖多，但今天除煩惱，明天除煩惱……，八萬四千煩惱總有消除的一天。

2. Continually improve and rid ourselves of delusions.

We all have many delusions. If we are persistent in sweeping our mind clean of delusions and are not frustrated by the enormity of the process, we will become enlightened one day.

第三，要自我實踐，不假外求：

佛法告訴我們，為人處事與修行都要靠自己去實踐，要自己守信、守時、守分、守約，不向外覓求。

3. Look to ourselves and not others to realize enlightenment.

The Dharma teaches us that we control our own destiny. How successful we are in life or in our spiritual practice depends on how diligently we work. We should do our part in everything over which we have direct influence. We should be trustworthy, punctual, content, and not always rely on others for help.

第四，要自我離相，不計勝負：

世人太執著於相，太愛在表面上、語言上、小事上斤斤計較。計較人我、得失、勝負，使我們天天陷溺於人我是非、得失的風波裡，不得安寧。因而我們要離一切相，離我相、人相、眾生相、壽者相，不被迷惑，不計勝負，進而臻於安身立命的境界。

4. Let go of our attachment to appearances and dualities.

Most of us are very attached to how things look or to what others may say about us. Because of this preoccupation, we become caught up with such dualities as self versus others, having versus not having, or winning versus losing. We constantly jockey for what we think is desirable and avoid what we think is not, creating much agony for ourselves and others in the process. To overcome this habitual tendency, we should let go of the notions of self and others. If we are at ease with our circumstances, then we will find peace and happiness in all that we do.

These suggestions are easier said than done. While it is hard to put them into practice, we should not give up. No one can do the work for us. We have to travel the road to enlightenment ourselves. Only then can we realize the truth of life.

以上「自悟修行」之道，看似容易，真正身體力行卻是一種自我的考驗，雖然不易實踐，但還是必須靠自己，任何人都無法替你開悟，替你修行。唯有自我的體悟，方能對人生有更加清明的領會。

自悟修行有四法：

第一，要自我觀照，反求諸己。

第二，要自我更新，不斷淨化。

第三、要自我實踐，不假外求。

第四、要自我離相，不計勝負。

In summary, there are four things we can do for ourselves to attain enlightenment. They are:

1. Use introspection and demand more of ourselves.
2. Continually improve and rid ourselves of delusions.
3. Look to ourselves and not others to realize enlightenment.
4. Let go of attachments to appearances and dualities.

如何修行　How to Practice

談修行，論修行，重要的是如何修行呢？可用四句偈十二種修行來做：

Although we often discuss the importance of practice, do we know how to proceed? The following four points comprise a verse that describes twelve ways to practice:

第一，修身修口修佛心：

首要是先修身，譬如不殺生、不偷盜、不邪淫、不打人、不亂做壞事，這就叫做修身。不妄語、不兩舌、不綺語、不誑語、不隨便亂說、不諷刺人、不傷害人，叫修口。最後還要修佛心，讓我們的心跟佛陀的心一樣，就是慈悲心、平等心、般若心。

1. Be mindful of our actions and speech and aware of our Buddha Nature.

A fundamental part of our practice is to be mindful of our actions. We should not harm others and should refrain from killing, stealing, and sexual misconduct. We should also not harm ourselves, for example by taking intoxicants.

In addition to our actions, we should also be mindful of our speech. We should not lie and gossip. We should not be boastful or slanderous of others. We should not engage in duplicity or spend our days in idle conversation. Last but not least, we should be aware of our Buddha Nature and walk in the path of Buddhas. We should nurture the minds of compassion, equanimity, and wisdom, or prajna.

第二，修自修他修人我：

把自己修健全了，叫修自。讓別人也得到利益，讓別人也漸漸地健全，好像父母教導兒女，老師教導子弟，這就叫做修他。修人我，是把人我的關係改善，大家和諧相處，這就要靠修養的工夫。

第三，修時修地修密行：

任何時候都可以修行，或一分鐘梵行，或五分鐘打坐，或十分鐘念佛禮拜。修行，就是在房間裡、客廳裡，不一定在佛堂，隨時隨地，舉心動念，皆可以修行。修密行，就是自己要有一點梵行，有一點密行，不一定要人家知道我有修行，我舉心動念都有密行。

2. Tend to our own cultivation, help others with theirs, and develop rapport with many.

Practice starts at home, so we should first be diligent in our own practice. If we are not spiritually strong ourselves, there is little chance that we can help others. Although we start with our own practice, we should not stop there for it is also important that we help others with theirs. As parents, we should teach our kids right from wrong. As teachers, we should educate our students well. As friends, we should help others see the beauty of the Dharma. Additionally, we should cultivate harmonious relationships with our family, neighbors, and friends.

3. Practice anytime, everywhere, and in all that we do.

We do not need to set aside a time or place to practice. We can make use of bits and pieces of time to practice, be it five minutes of sitting meditation here or ten minutes of reciting the name of Buddha there. We can practice anywhere, be it in the bedroom or living room. We can make every thought and every act our practice. As long as we apply the right effort, it is not important that our practice appears obvious.

50

第四，修福修慧修禪淨：

造福人群，利益別人，叫修福。修慧，就是自己要有靈巧、智慧、聰明，能悟道。修福修慧，福慧雙修，再修禪、修淨土皆可。

十二種修行法門，就是：

第一，修身修口修佛心。

第二，修自修他修人我。

第三，修時修地修密行。

第四，修福修慧修禪淨。

4. Extend kindness, cultivate wisdom, and practice the Chan or Pure Land way.

When we do something nice for others, we are giving others happiness and cultivating blessings for ourselves. When we calm the mind, we are cultivating wisdom so that we may develop the insight for enlightenment. Both the Chan and Pure Land schools teach us many ways to extend kindness and cultivate wisdom.

The twelve ways of practice are:

1. Be mindful of our actions and speech and aware of our Buddha Nature.
2. Tend to our own cultivation, help others with theirs, and develop rapport with many.
3. Practice anytime, everywhere, and in all that we do.
4. Extend kindness, cultivate wisdom, and practice the Chan or Pure Land way.

如何修持身口意

有時候我們講修身，有時候我們講修口，有時候我們講修心、修意，究竟要如何修持身、口、意呢？

We create karma through the three doors of karma: body, speech, and thought. How do we stay vigilant of them so that we do not create unwholesome karma? I have a few suggestions:

第一，身常行慈，不殺不盜不淫：

我們身體所犯的罪惡之中，最嚴重的就是殺生、竊盜、邪淫，也就是殺、盜、淫。殺人、傷害、打人，是犯法的啊！竊盜、搶劫、綁票、侵占，也都是犯罪的，甚至於邪淫、不正當的感情。有傷風化、妨害家庭、拐騙等，都是罪惡。如果身常行慈，不殺、不盜、不淫，就是身的修行了。

1. Practice compassion of the body: abstain from killing, stealing, and sexual misconduct.

The most serious offenses the body can commit are killing, stealing, and sexual misconduct. We all know that killing another person is wrong, but we need to expand the meaning of killing to include assault or other injurious behavior. Cruelty to animals is another example of killing. Stealing, robbing, and kidnapping are serious crimes. Sexual misconduct can include dressing seductively or having an adulterous affair. These behaviors can hurt those involved and break up families.

第二，口常行慈，不妄不假不騙：

口舌，最容易造罪業，假話說成真的，是妄語；真的說成假的，挑撥離間，是兩舌。「一言興邦，一言喪邦」，口，能像刀劍

2. Practice compassion of speech: abstain from slandering, lying, and cheating.

Very often we create unwholesome karma with our speech without even knowing it. When we start

傷人；口，也能做功德，口，也
能修行。有時候我們讚美別人幾
句，卻產生無窮的影響力，所以
我們要多多用口修行，不妄語，
不說假話，不欺騙人。

第三，意常行慈，不貪不瞋不痴：
　　貪、瞋、痴稱為三毒，是我們學
佛的三種障道因緣，由於它能毒
害我們心中的善法，使我們長劫
受苦而不得出離，因此學佛首先
要去除貪瞋痴。如果我們的心中
充滿貪欲、瞋恨、邪見、愚痴，
就像杯子裡裝滿了髒水，如何能
接受清淨的甘露法水呢？所以出
家人稱為「沙門」，亦即「勤息」
的意思，也就是說要勤修戒定
慧，息滅貪瞋痴。因此修行要常
行慈悲，要不貪、不瞋、不痴。

malicious rumors about others, we commit slander. Lying is not telling the whole truth about something or distorting the truth. Duplicity in speech is also a form of lying. There is a Chinese saying, A simple word can make or break a country. If we are not careful with what we say, words can hurt like knives. Words can also heal and bring peace. A few words of encouragement can have a huge influence on others. We should use our words wisely.

3. Practice compassion of thought: abstain from greed, hatred, and delusion.

　　Greed, hatred, and delusion are the three poisons of the mind and are hindrances to our practice. They cover up our pure nature and keep us in the cycle of rebirth. When the mind is filled with these three poisons, there is little chance to hold any clean water. We have to root out these three poisons. To do this, we should observe the precepts, calm the mind, and develop wisdom.

發心（一）

我們經常聽到佛教徒勸人要發心，發心很重要。發心不是佛教徒的專利，社會上任何一個人都可以發心。比方說：我們發心吃飯，飯菜會特別甜美；發心睡覺，覺會睡得很安穩；做事更要發心，發心便不畏艱難辛苦。所以心一發，無事不成。但要發什麼心呢？

第一，發慈悲心，人我無間：

佛教講「無緣大慈，同體大悲」。有慈悲心的人必能泯滅人我對待，必能不分親疏的照顧到週遭的人，自然能與別人沒有隔閡，達到人我無間。

Initiating the Mind (I)

Initiating the mind means committing oneself to a goal or making a vow. We often hear Chinese Buddhists advise people to initiate the mind and how important it is to do so. The act of initiating the mind is not confined to Buddhists alone; anyone in society can do the same. For instance, if people's minds are committed to eating good food, they will find their food particularly delicious. Likewise, people will find sleep especially sound if their minds are committed to sleeping. When we embark on anything, we should initiate the mind. In this way we will have no fear of any hardships or obstacles. When we initiate the mind, we can do almost anything. How should we initiate the mind?

1. Initiate the mind with compassion to maintain effortless relationships with others.

To practice the Dharma we should be kind regardless of circumstances. We should have compassion for others as we do for ourselves, as if we were all one. A person with a mind of compassion can transcend all duality and help those in distress regardless of conditions. In this way, we are not at a distance from others and maintain all relationships effortlessly.

第二，發信願心，常隨佛學：

常隨佛學是普賢菩薩所發的十大願之一。我們學佛，就是要學習佛菩薩的發心立願，我們要常跟隨善知識、老師、大德們學習，有一份發心必有一番成就。

2. Initiate the mind with faith to continually learn from the Buddhas.

One of the Samantabhadra Bodhisattva's ten great vows is to continually learn from the Buddhas. To learn from the Buddhas is to learn from their practice of initiating the mind and making vows. We should associate with and learn from the learned, teachers, and people of great virtue. If we can initiate the mind, we are bound to succeed.

第三，發菩提心，上弘下化：

菩提心就是「上求佛道，下化眾生」的一種願心。這是學佛的人都應該發的大心，能發菩提心，必能進趣菩薩道。

3. Initiate the mind in the way of the bodhisattva to spread the Dharma and show the way to all beings.

The bodhi mind vows to seek the way of the Buddhas and show the way to all sentient beings. All who follow the way should initiate the mind in the way of the bodhisattva. If we can initiate our minds thusly, we will find the bodhisattvas way.

第四，發無我心，擴大完成：

所謂無我，並不是指人死了以後，什麼都沒有了。無我是說我們的心境可以包容一切，將別人看成與自己一樣，為了完成大

4. Initiate the mind with selfless effort to strive for the greater good.

To be selfless does not mean to cease existence at the time of death. The term selfless is used to des-

我，而可以犧牲小我。能夠發無
我的心，把自己融入大眾，融入
團體，那麼大眾就是我，團體就
是我。所以無我之我，反而更
大、更高，更能成就一切，完成
一切。

所以，為成就自己，每個人應該
發心：

第一，發慈悲心，人我無間。

第二，發信願心，常隨佛學。

第三，發菩提心，上弘下化。

第四，發無我心，擴大完成。

cribe the mental state of being able
to encompass everything, being able
to view others as we would ourselves, and being able to sacrifice
one s self for the greater good. If we
can initiate the mind in selfless
effort, then we will be able to participate in society and in the com-
munity. In this way, we become lar-
ger than our solitary selves and will
be capable of fulfilling greater tasks.

**Thus, for our own fulfillment, we
should initiate our minds:**

1. With compassion to maintain
   effortless relationships with
   others.
2. With faith to continually learn
   from the Buddhas.
3. In the way of the bodhisattva to
   spread the Dharma and show the
   way to all beings.
4. With selfless effort to strive for
   the greater good.

發心（二）

Initiating the Mind (II)

發心，就是立志，就是發願。發心是動力，無論什麼機器都要講究它的動力有多少，我們每一個人所發的心有多大，它的動力就有多大。如何發心呢？有四點意見：

There are numerous ways in which to initiate the mind. What does initiating the mind mean? It means being committed to a goal, making a vow. Initiating the mind is a source of power. When we talk about a piece of machinery, we want to know how much power it has. When one initiates one s own mind, its power depends on how strong our commitment is. We have already mentioned four ways to initiate the mind. Below are four more suggestions:

第一，恥有所不知的發心：

慚愧自己有很多不知道，比方說很多的科技常識我不知道，很多的文學典故我不懂，很多的哲學理論我不明白，甚至於做人處事的道理，我都不健全，因而感到慚愧，感到可恥。因為恥於自己不知道，才會激勵自己發心學習。所以要廣學多聞，要博覽一切常識，不會駕駛的就去學開車，不會電腦的就去學習資訊，不會記帳的就去學習會計帳目，不會音樂唱歌的就去學習各種樂器等。

1. Initiate the mind with wisdom and be disdainful of our own ignorance.

We should feel regret for what we do not know. When we regret our ignorance in science and technology, in the field of literature, and philosophical discourse, and even in the ways of getting along well with people, then we will have motivation to learn. We should strive to broaden our knowledge and experience, and to read extensively on all kinds of subjects. One who does not drive should take driving lessons; one who does not know about computers should learn; one who does not know about accounting should learn bookkeeping; and one who does not know about music should learn to play a musical instrument.

第二，恥有所不能的發心：

慚愧自己有很多不能，譬如我做事不周全，我教書不能盡職，我領導人不盡圓滿。慚愧自己的無能，因此要發心，增強自己的能力，以便能擔當負責。

2. Initiate the mind with skillfulness and be disdainful of our own incompetence.

When we realize our incompetence in all fields, in the way we deal with others, in our inability to teach, or in our lack of leadership skills, then we can resolve to improve our skills so that we can shoulder more responsibility.

第三，恥有所不淨的發心：

慚愧自己的心地不清淨，心裏常常充滿貪瞋煩惱，常常有侵犯別人的意念，常常心懷陰謀詭計，充滿種種貪欲等。因此，要發心來改善自己、淨化自己。

3. Initiate the mind with purity and be disdainful of that which is impure.

We should be remorseful about our impure minds, of the times when our minds are filled with greed, anger, afflictions, aggression toward others, and scheming thoughts. Thus, we can commit our minds to turning over a new leaf, mending our ways, and purifying our being.

第四，恥有所不善的發心：

慚愧自己有很多不好的地方，譬如沒有盡力去做善事，所以今後要多發心多做一點善事，多布施自己的錢財，多帶給別人歡喜。

4. Initiate the mind with virtue and be disdainful of that which is not virtuous.

We should feel remorse about our shortcomings. If we have not exerted ourselves to participate in charitable works, then we should commit the mind to do more charity, to make donations, and to bring happiness to others.

所以如何發心？就是：

第一，恥有所不知的發心。

第二，恥有所不能的發心。

第三，恥有所不淨的發心。

第四，恥有所不善的發心。

How do we initiate our minds? We should:

1. Initiate the mind with wisdom and be disdainful of our own ignorance.
2. Initiate the mind with skillfulness and be disdainful of our own incompetence.
3. Initiate the mind with purity and be disdainful of that which is impure.
4. Initiate the mind with virtue and be disdainful of that which is not virtuous.

交朋友一定要交有德的朋友。

如果我們所交往的對象都能影響我們做善事、發善心...

...Friends who have a positive influence over us and can help us act wholesomely are good role models...

如何認識真理

How to Recognize Truth

真理就是諸法實相。有人說，真理是不容易認識的！現在佛法裡面還是有方法可以認識真理。我提供四點意見：

What is truth? Truth is the reality of all phenomena. Some of you may say it is hard to recognize and see the truth! Buddhism teaches us how to recognize truth, and I am going to offer four points in this regard.

第一，用正見來認識善惡：

所謂正見，就是如實地了知世間與出世間的因果，也就是正確的認識有善有惡、有業有報、有聖人有凡夫、有前生有來世。具足正確的見解能使我們認識真理，明白善惡。

1. Use right perception to recognize truth.

With the right perception, we will be able to correctly comprehend the law of cause and effect. We will be able to see that there is goodness and evil, karma and consequence, the enlightened and yet-to-be enlightened, and there is this life and a future life. With the right perception, we will be able to recognize truth and discern right from wrong.

第二，用般若來判斷真假：

世間上，所謂真真假假、假假真真，誰是真？誰是假？誰是對？誰是錯？必須要用般若來判斷。般若就是明見一切事物及道理的高深智慧，它不同於一般的世智辯聰，世俗的聰明智慧，有時候也會做錯。比方說犯罪，有所謂的智慧型，可見聰明智慧也是不究竟的，它只是一種知識的

2. Use wisdom, or prajna, to distinguish truth from falsehood.

What is truth? What is falsehood? Who is right? Who is wrong? To make correct assessments, we must use prajna. Prajna is the highest form of wisdom with which we can see and understand the workings of the world around us. Prajna is different from worldly intellect and wit. Intelligence and smartness are just the culmination of

累積；知識有時候也會生病而成為愚痴，所以知字上面加個病字頭，就是痴。因此，只有用般若的純淨智慧，才能認清世間上的真真假假、假假真真。

knowledge. Knowledge can also lead us astray. In fact, some criminals are very intelligent individuals. The Chinese character for the word delusion is the combination of two characters knowledge and sickness. Only when we use the pure wisdom of prajna can we distinguish truth from falsehood.

第三，用法印來抉擇是非：

世間上到處充滿了是非，此亦是非，彼亦是非，就以宗教界來說，也是公說公有理，婆說婆有理。究竟誰是真理？其實不必爭論，可以用法來「印」證誰是真理。佛教講真理必須合於「普遍如此、本來如此、必然如此」的條件。也就是說，一個道理必須是普遍如此，不能說在這裡有理，在那裡無理；在你有理，在他就沒有理，這就不合於真理的條件，所以真理是普遍如此的，是必然如此的，是本來如此的。比方說因果，有因就有果，又比如生死，有生就有死，這是誰也改變不了的。所以，我們要用法印來抉擇是非。

3. Use the Dharma to assess right from wrong.

How do we tell right from wrong? Even in the world of religions, every religion claims to represent truth. Who is right? Actually, we do not need to debate this, because the Dharma can help us. Buddhism teaches us that truth must be in accordance with conditions. If truth is considered to apply only under the condition that it originally was like this, it inevitably is like this, or that it is applicable only in a certain country or to a certain group of people, then it is not the truth. Take the law of cause and effect; every cause will yield an effect. Take the example of birth and death; every birth will eventually lead to death. These are immutable laws that can never be changed. Thus, we can use the Dharma to help us assess right from wrong.

第四，用空理來體會有無：

世間上什麼叫有？什麼叫無？佛教講的「空」可以把有和無都統攝起來，因為空理中含蘊著因緣聚有和因緣散無。

所以如何認識真理？就是：

第一，用正見來認識善惡。

第二，用般若來判斷真假。

第三，用法印來抉擇是非。

第四，用空理來體會有無。

4. Use sunyata (emptiness) to comprehend existence and non-existence.

What is existence? What is non-existence? When we truly understand sunyata, we will see that existence and non-existence are one and the same. The concept of sunyata teaches us that existence arises when the right conditions come together and ceases when the right conditions no longer prevail.

How do we recognize truth? We can:

1. Use right perception to recognize truth.
2. Use wisdom, or prajna, to distinguish truth from falsehood.
3. Use the Dharma to assess right from wrong.
4. Use sunyata (emptiness) to comprehend existence and non-existence.

如何觀照

人，往往只看到別人，看不到
自己。由於自我的觀照不夠，因
此產生煩惱。假如我們懂得觀照
自己，常常自我反省、自我健
全，修持「五停心」，就能對治煩
惱了。以下介紹五種對治煩惱的
觀照方法：

第一，以不淨觀對治貪欲：

我們的貪欲是怎麼生起的？就
是「愛」，有愛就有貪心。假如你
有不淨觀，就能減低貪念。比方
說：貪圖金錢，想到金錢有時候
會引人犯罪；迷戀愛情，愛情會
帶給你負擔、煩惱；你有美貌，
美貌也只是帶肉的骷髏。有了不
淨觀，就不會受染污，你的貪
美、貪愛、貪財之心就會減少
了。

Contemplation

It is often said in Buddhism that
contemplation can help us eradicate
delusion. The most common contemplations are the contemplations
of impurity, compassion, conditionality, breathing, and of a Buddha s name.

**1. Contemplate impurity to calm
the mind of greed.**

How does greed arise? Greed
comes from attachment. When
there is attachment, there is greed.
How does the contemplation of
impurities calm the mind of greed?
Take the example of the greed for
wealth. When we watch others win
the lottery, we feel a tinge of jealousy and wish we were in the shoes
of the winners. Actually, wealth can
become a source of headaches.
Many people who have come into
sudden wealth conclude that their
lives were changed forever, and not
necessarily for the better. They start
to worry about the possibility of
being kidnapped. They are hounded
by charities that want a share of
their new-found wealth.

As for love, when we are blind-
ly in love, we begin to worry that

our lovers will leave us. Beauty can also bring us worries. Beauty is only skin-deep and does not last forever. If we contemplate the impurities of these worldly pursuits, our attachments to wealth, love, or appearance will be lessened.

第二，以慈悲觀對治瞋恨：

瞋恨是三毒之一，瞋恨心也是來自貪愛，所謂由愛生恨，人一有了貪愛之心，就想執取、占有，萬一欲望得不到滿足，就會生起瞋恨心。假如我們能用慈悲觀來對治，就是我凡事給你歡喜，給你幫助，我就不會瞋恨你了。

2. Contemplate compassion to calm the mind of hatred.

Hatred is one of the three poisons of the mind. Hatred comes from greed and attachment. It is often said that love breeds hatred. When we love a person too much, our love turns into a desire to possess the other person. If this desire is not satisfied, we become filled with jealousy or hatred for the other person. Compassion is the purest form of love. Compassion is giving to others, without expecting anything in return. When love matures into compassion, there is no room for hatred to grow.

第三，以因緣觀對治愚痴：

人類由於不明白世間上的事物，都是因緣所成，因此產生執著。執著於我的親人、我的財富、我的身體，因為執著，產生了無明、煩惱，這就是愚痴，這就是不能認識事物的真相。如果你懂得因緣，就會知道眾緣和合

3. Contemplate conditionality to eradicate ignorance.

Ignorance is not understanding that all worldly phenomena arise and cease because of causes and conditions. One sutra states, When this arises, that arises; when this ceases, that ceases. Because we do not understand the nature of dependent origination, we do not know

的奧妙，就能轉愚痴為智慧。

that all phenomena are inherently impermanent and that we should let go of our attachments. We become attached to our bodies, wealth, health, and success. When our circumstances change, we are at a loss as to what to do. If we contemplate conditionality, we will have a sense of peace with any circumstances in which we find ourselves.

第四，以數息觀對治散亂：

　　我們的散亂心，可以用數息觀來對治。就是把心念集中在計數自己的呼吸上，從一呼一吸中，把我們的心安定下來。

4. Contemplate breathing to calm the wandering mind.

　　Our mind is like a wild horse running in all directions. We can calm the mind by contemplating breathing. When we concentrate on our breathing, as we inhale and exhale, we can gradually calm the wandering mind.

第五，以念佛觀對治煩惱：

　　我們的煩惱很多，煩惱主要來自於妄想雜念。假如我們能一心念佛，讓一句句「阿彌陀佛、阿彌陀佛」、「觀音菩薩、觀音菩薩」的佛號在心中持續不斷，就會達到一種無念的境界，就能去除煩惱，這就是以正念來對治妄念。

所以觀照自己的方法有五點：

5. Contemplate the name of a Buddha to eradicate delusion.

　　We have many worries, and most of them come from our deluded understanding of the world. When we focus our energies to say the name of Amitabha Buddha or Avalokitesvara Bodhisattva, we are essentially replacing a deluded thought with a pure thought. In this way, we calm the agitation in the mind and root out our worries.

第一，以不淨觀對治貪欲。

第二，以慈悲觀對治瞋恨。

第三，以因緣觀對治愚痴。

第四，以數息觀對治散亂。

第五，以念佛觀對治煩惱。

**The five ways to calm the mind
and reflect on ourselves are:**
1. Contemplate impurity to calm
   the mind of greed.
2. Contemplate compassion to
   calm the mind of hatred.
3. Contemplate conditionality to
   eradicate ignorance.
4. Contemplate breathing to calm
   the wandering mind.
5. Contemplate the name of a Buddha to eradicate delusion.

善知識的條件

一個人找老師，一定要找好老師；交朋友一定要交有德的朋友。如果我們所交往的對象都能影響我們做善事、發善心，這就是值得我們交往的善知識。善知識的條件有四：

第一，要有悲憫的心懷：

所交的朋友、老師不但要有慈悲心、憐憫心，而且要有入俗的心懷，有普利的胸襟，對我都講些讓我向上、向善的話，勉勵我為聖、為賢。

第二，要有正直的性格：

所交的朋友，所找的老師如果是諂佞、不正直，就是不好的朋友。好的師友必須要有真心、直心，《維摩經》裡講「直心是道場」，誠實、正直才是善知識。

What to Look For in a Role Model

When we look for a teacher, we look for a qualified teacher. In the matter of making friends, we should befriend those who have a good personality and character. Friends who have a positive influence over us and can help us act wholesomely are good role models. So, what do we look for in a role model? A good role model is someone who is:

1. Compassionate

The friends we make should be kind and compassionate. They should be willing to reach out to all kinds of people and encourage others to do the same. They are encouraging, always motivating others around them to excel and to do good deeds.

2. Honest and righteous

Friends who are coniving in their character, insincere, and dishonest are not good friends. A good friend is someone who is honest and righteous. The *Vimalakirti Sutra* says, Righteousness is a display of the Dharma. We should emulate those who are honest and righteous.

第三，要有明辨的慧巧：

　　我的朋友、老師要能明辨是非，分別善惡，有權衡輕重的慧巧。如果我的朋友、老師或與之有交往者都無法做到上述的條件，那我與他相處必定也受影響。

第四，要有公正的態度：

　　朋友、老師的做人處事，要能公正、公平，所有一切都能公開，我和這樣的朋友來往，必定受其利。即使沒有朋友的相助，自己本身也要努力做到這種善知識的條件。

因此，善知識的條件，就是：

第一，要有悲憫的心懷。
第二，要有正直的性格。

3. Judicious

Our friends and teachers should possess the ability to discern right from wrong or good from bad. If our friends and teachers cannot exercise proper judgement, then we also stand the chance of being led astray.

4. Objective and impartial

Our friends and teachers should be fair and objective in how they deal with other people. They should not be secretive and keep others in the dark about what they are up to. If we make friends with those who are objective and impartial, we can learn to be the same. Even if we are not able to find friends who have these qualities, we should strive to live up to these standards.

Thus, a good role model is someone who is:

1. Compassionate
2. Honest and righteous
3. Judicious
4. Objective and impartial

出世的思想

Transcendence

我們常聽說先要有出世的思想，再辦入世的事業。什麼叫「出世的思想」呢？

We often hear that in our cultivation our perspectives should be transcendental, yet we should be worldly in the way we interact with others. What does transcendence mean? There are four aspects:

第一，對人生要有無常的警覺：

人生非常短暫，歲月總在我們的疏忽間一去不回，千萬不要誤以為孝順父母，報答恩情來日方長。人不能醉生夢死，對於人生，如果有無常的警覺，什麼事就應立即去做，不延遲，以出世的思想來增加我們入世的精神。

1. Be vigilant about impermanence.

Life is short and fragile; if we are not vigilant about how we use our time, months will turn into years, and before we know it, many years will have passed by. We must not think that there is always time for us to show our gratitude for what our parents have done for us. One day, we will wake up only to find that our parents have passed away, and we have not done our part to love and take care of them. How sad this would be! We must not live lackadaisical lives, drifting through life aimlessly. If we are vigilant about the impermanence of life, then we will not procrastinate on the things that need to be done today.

第二，對物質要有遠離的看法：

物質會引起我們的欲望，讓我們生起貪念的心。物質是有窮盡的，欲望是無窮盡的，所以被物

2. Be free of materialistic attachments.

Materialistic attachments are often the genesis of our desire. When our desires are out of control,

質引誘，苦海越陷越深。假如我們對物質有遠離的看法，有不受物累，不被物質束縛的出世思想，如此才能更放開胸襟，為國家、社會、人類謀取幸福。

we become prisoners of material comforts and the hold material possessions have on us grows tighter and tighter. If we can have material possessions without any attachments, they will not control us. This kind of outlook is what we mean by transcendence. This kind of perspective can help us broaden our minds, enabling us to work for the welfare of all sentient beings.

第三，對情愛要有淡化的觀念：

由於情愛的執著，所以就有許多感情上的煩惱和困擾。如果我們能把愛情昇華，以夫妻相愛的感情來愛我們的父母、朋友，乃至社會、國家，那麼，因情愛所發生的問題自然就會減少。私愛越淡，對社會國家的大愛就會增長。

3. Be expansive in the way we love.

Much of the agony and despair in personal relationships is due to our attachments to emotion. If we can expand our love for a few to a love that embraces our parents, friends, and the whole human race, then many of our love-related problems will disappear. The less selfish our love is, the more we can love others.

第四，對自己要有不滿的要求：

人常常是苛責別人，原諒自己的。如果反過來對自己有不滿的要求，覺得自己不清淨、不慈悲，覺得自己的修養還不夠，就會更加發奮上進，更能為別人設想。

4. Have high expectations of ourselves.

Most of us tend to expect much from others, but easily overlook our own faults and flaws. If we can, instead, be more demanding of ourselves than others, then we will strive to improve. We should continually expect ourselves to become more compassionate, enlightened, and considerate of others.

所以，出世的思想，有四點要明白：

第一，對人生要有無常的警覺。

第二，對物質要有遠離的看法。

第三，對情愛要有淡化的觀念。

第四，對自己要有不滿的要求。

In summary, to develop a trans-cendental outlook on life means that we should:

1. Be vigilant about imperman-ence.
2. Be free of materialistic attach-ments.
3. Be expansive in the way we love.
4. Have high expectations of our-selves.

無常的價值

在一般人的思想觀念裡，大都不喜歡無常。總覺得人生無常，令人恐懼；人情無常，令人悲傷；世界無常，成住壞空；一切無常，虛假如幻。所以一談到無常，往往認為是消極的、悲觀的、沒有意義的。但從另一層面來看，無常實際上是蘊含著積極奮發的思想。所以，對於無常的價值，我們應該有如下的幾點看法：

第一，帶來希望的人生：

無常的定義是：好的會變壞，壞的會變好。所以它帶給我們無窮的希望，它讓我們懂得珍惜美好的，改善不好的。譬如現在我貧窮，沒有關係，貧窮是無常的，我可以努力，總有一天我會成功的！一旦我有錢了，我也知道要好好惜福，因為我知道無常，如果不好好愛惜，千萬金錢

The Value of Impermanence

Most of us cringe at the mention of impermanence and what it entails. We usually associate impermanence with unpleasant experiences. When we think of impermanence in the context of friendship, we envision friends leaving us. When we say that the world is impermanent, we automatically think of decay and destruction. When we describe everything as impermanent, we feel at a loss. The word impermanence usually elicits a sense of doom and gloom. But if we just pause for a minute and look at impermanence from another angle, we will realize that impermanence can also embody hope. We should learn to see the value of impermanence.

1. Impermanence gives us hope.

Impermanence means that the good can change for the worse, and vice versa. The bad can improve for the better. As such, impermanence gives us hope; impermanence is what makes improvement possible. As an example, suppose I am poor now. If I can look at my economic condition from the standpoint of impermanence, I would not be bothered by the fact that I am poor.

也會隨流水而去。在情感上，你愛我，我會珍惜，你對我不好，沒關係，我來改善不好的前因，未來我們就有希望結成善緣。

The state of poverty is impermanent; I can work hard, and one day I will succeed! And, if I become financially secure, I should then cherish my blessings, for wealth is also impermanent. If I do not use my money wisely, it can disappear like the wind. The same also applies to relationships. If someone loves you, you should cherish his or her love. If someone does not trust you, you should accept it and work hard to improve the relationship, so that you can be friends one day.

第二，具有自由的精神：

無常的另一個定義是，凡事都不是命定的。因此，每個人都可以自由的改變自己的命運。我可以從改變處世的方法等種種改變上，來扭轉原有的命運，這種改變，是我能你能，大家都能的。因為無常是人人平等的，無論你是國王大臣，還是販夫走卒，無常一樣跟你在一起。所以大家都可好可壞，可壞可好，這是很平等的。

第三，否定神權的控制：

人活著，最苦惱的就是對自己的未來茫然無知，因此很容易被神權控制，很容易把自己的未來交給神權去主宰。但是如果明白

2. Impermanence gives us freedom.

Impermanence means that life is not predestined. Each one of us has the freedom to determine the course of our life. We can, for example, change our attitude toward others in order to change our circumstances. Such change is something that we are all capable of doing. In terms of impermanence, we all are equal, regardless of social status or who we know. We all can change for the better or for the worse.

3. Impermanence offers us control.

One of the worst fears in life is the fear of not knowing what the future holds. It is the easiest not to be concerned with the future,

無常的道理，就會肯定自己的未來，就能脫離神權思想的控制，而做自己因緣的主人。

leaving it in the hands of some gods. If we understand the truth of impermanence, then we know that we are the masters of our own future.

第四，破除定命的論調：

　　剛才說過，凡事都不是命定的，命運是操縱在自己的手中，所以只要我們心好，只要我們不侵犯別人，而又能廣結善緣，無常亦能使乖舛的命運轉好。

4. Impermanence refutes predestination.

Our life is not predestined. There is no such thing as destiny; our future is in our own hands. If we approach life with good intentions, refrain from harming others, and treat others with kindness, our lives will change for the better.

所以無常的價值，就是：

第一，帶來希望的人生。
第二，具有自由的精神。
第三，否定神權的控制。
第四，破除定命的論調。

What is the value of impermanence?

1. Impermanence gives us hope.
2. Impermanence gives us freedom.
3. Impermanence offers us control.
4. Impermanence refutes predestination.

修道者的行儀

我們經常看到一些修道人，他們莊嚴的儀表，令人一見就忍不住心生景仰、讚美，這就是佛教所講的威儀。佛教裡有所謂「行如風，立如松，坐如鐘，臥如弓」的四威儀，也就是說，行走的時候要像一陣風般的輕快敏捷，站的時候要像古松般地正直挺拔，坐的時候要像大鐘般地沉穩莊重，睡覺的時候要像彎弓般地右脅而臥，也就是所謂的吉祥臥。另外有一首佛教偈語，也是關於行儀的，今天把它介紹給大家：

Decorum

When we see practioners carry themselves with grace and decorum, we naturally feel a sense of respect for them. There is a saying that it is not the clothes that make the man, but it is the way we carry ourselves that shows others who we are. Within the Buddhist tradition, grace and decorum are also important parts of one s practice. This is a short verse that helps us stay mindful of this element of our practice:

> *Walk like the wind,*
> *Stand like a pine,*
> *Sit like a bell,*
> *Recline like a bow.*

When we walk, we should not drag our feet but walk with the flair of a gentle breeze. When we stand, we should stand tall like a pine tree. When we sit, it is important that we sit still and steady like a heavy bell. When we lie down to rest, we should sleep on the right side of the body, like we see in pictures of the Buddha entering parinirvana.

「舉佛音聲慢水流，

　誦經行道雁行遊；

　合掌當胸如捧水，

　立身頂上似安油；

　瞻前顧後輕移步，

　左右迴旋半展眸；

　威儀動靜常如此，

　不愧佛門修行人。」

　　這就是說，念佛的音聲要像海潮音一般，輕輕柔柔、細細緩緩的，彷彿是涓涓滴滴的慢慢流著。「誦經行道雁行遊」，是說誦經的時候，或者是繞佛走路的時候，要像天上的飛雁，很規律、很整齊的排列成行，而不是散亂漫走。「合掌當胸如捧水」，合掌的時候，要像手中捧著水一般的謹慎，不可以鬆散而失去威儀。「立身頂上似安油」，站著的時

In addition to the above verse, there is a longer one that can help us visualize proper demeanor. It goes like this:

Say the Buddha's name with a
*　voice like a gentle stream.*
Recite sutras and walk in
*　meditation, as geese fly*
*　together.*
Join palms before the chest as if
*　carrying water.*
Stand tall as if carrying a bowl
*　of oil on the head.*
Walk lightly, look ahead, and be
*　mindful of what's behind.*
Turn not your head from side to
*　side.*
Carry yourself with grace and
*　dignity thus,*
You deserve to be called a
*　Buddhist practitioner.*

When we say the Buddha's name, our voice should be soft and flowing like a gentle stream. When we recite the sutras or circumambulate a Buddha statue, we should do so in an orderly manner. When geese fly, they do so in formation and with discipline. When we join palms before the chest, we should not be lackadaisical. When we stand, we should stand still as if carrying a bowl of oil on the head. Many models train to walk elegantly by placing a book on the head. In

候，要像頭頂著一碗油，昂首而立，如如不動。如同現在中國小姐、世界小姐，如果要訓練她們走路，也會讓她們頭上頂著東西走，才能走出萬千儀態來。「瞻前顧後輕移步，左右迴旋半展眸」，就是說走路的時候要觀前顧後，慢慢的一步一步走，但不可以東張西望，縱然左右有一些你想知道的事，也只能半展眸，約略知道就好了。威儀動靜能夠如此，就不會慚愧自己是佛門中的修行人了。所以，如果我們想成為一個很有威儀的人，應該把這一首佛門行儀的詩歌牢記在心——

「舉佛音聲慢水流，
　　誦經行道雁行遊；
　合掌當胸如捧水，
　　立身頂上似安油；
　瞻前顧後輕移步，
　　左右迴旋半展眸；
　威儀動靜常如此，
　　不愧佛門修行人。」

walking, we should look ahead but not forget what is behind us. We should stay focused and not become easily distracted by what is happening around us.

Some people may think that these rules of etiquette are outdated and not suitable for the twenty-first century. The purpose of these rules of etiquette is to help us work on our practice from the outside in. By calming the body, we learn to calm the mind. The two reinforce one another. When we carry ourselves with grace and dignity, our practice will also improve.

道不一定在佛祖那裡，
道也不一定在出家人那裡；
道應該是在每一個人的眼前，
每一個人的身邊，每一個人的心裡。

...The Way is not necessarily to be found in a Buddha statue or at a monastery. The Way is always in front of our eyes. It is right beside us and in our minds...

道在那裡

常常聽人說：他要修道、學道。但道在何處？道不一定在佛祖那裡，道也不一定在出家人那裡；道應該是在每一個人的眼前，每一個人的身邊，每一個人的心裡，所以自己要有道。要有什麼道呢？

第一，學習接受，是自我充實之道：

現在的青年學生，為什麼有些人讀書進步，有些人讀書沒有進步，原因何在？在於他沒有學習接受，臺上老師講課，他在臺下神遊；父母說的經驗談，兒女並沒有受教；長官講的連篇道理，他也沒有接受。所以，一個人要自我充實，要自我進步，要自我有道，在學習的時候，就必須要接受，認真的聽講還要聽得透徹。佛教中有言：「以聞思修而入三摩地。」意思是聽了以後要思，思了以後還要修，所以這個接受就有道。

Where is the Way

We have often heard people say, I want to learn how to cultivate the Way. But, where is the Way? The Way is not necessarily to be found in a Buddha statue or at a monastery. The Way is always in front of our eyes. It is right beside us and in our minds. What is this Way that we seek?

1. To learn from others is the Way of self-improvement.

Why do some students learn easily while others fail to show signs of progress? The problem is that some students do not want help and guidance from others. When in the classroom, they daydream. When their parents share their life experience with them, they turn a deaf ear. When their supervisors give them advice, they refuse to listen. If one wants to improve oneself, one must know the right way to learn. When others teach us, we should have the right attitude toward learning. We should pay attention and test our understanding to make sure that our understanding is correct and thorough. In Buddhism, there is a saying, To enter samadhi, one must listen, contemplate, and practice. This is the Way to learn.

第二，想當然爾，是自在安忍之道：

現在的人，有好意見時總是唱反調；但一個有為者，老師罵他、打他，他會覺得理所當然，因為這是教育；父母責怪他，長官批評他的種種不是，他都認為這是理所當然，這就是自在安忍之道。

第三，凡事忍耐，是自由快樂之道：

一切事情都要忍耐，忍耐就是力量。現今，有的人就是不能忍耐，即使是一點點不順意也叫苦連天，也要反彈，因此他就不能自由快樂，不能擔當。

第四，讚美別人，是自己善緣之道：

常說好話，讚美別人，人家喜歡，自己也歡喜。所以讚美別人，自己就有道，就是結緣之道。

2. To accept things as they are is the Way of peace and tranquility.

If we can accept things as they are, then we will not be cynical when our teacher disciplines us. After all, it is the role of the teacher to discipline a student when necessary. Parents are supposed to educate and sometimes reprimand their children. Supervisors are supposed to critique our work. When we can understand our role and the roles of others, we will be at peace.

3. To have patience and tolerance is the Way of happiness.

One needs to be patient and tolerant, for tolerance is a source of power. Nowadays, tolerance is in short supply. When we are faced with a little hardship, we complain without end. If we do not learn to be tolerant, we cannot shoulder great responsibilities and will remain unhappy.

4. To speak well of others is the Way to build good relationships.

If we are generous with our praise and give credit where credit is due, we will make others happy, which in turn will make ourselves happy. Thus, to speak well of others is the Way to build good relationships.

道在那裡？

第一，學習接受，是自我充實之道。
第二，想當然爾，是自在安忍之道。
第三，凡事忍耐，是自由快樂之道。
第四，讚美別人，是自己善緣之道。

So, where is the Way?

1. To learn from others is the Way of self-improvement.

2. To accept things as they are is the Way of peace and tranquility.

3. To have patience and tolerance is the Way of happiness.

4. To speak well of others is the Way to build good relationships.

什麼是佛道

所謂「佛道」，就是佛教的真理。什麼是佛教的真理？我提出四點意見：

第一，自由業力是佛道：

佛教和一般宗教不同的地方，就是佛教不講究由一個神明來控制自我，不主張另有天神賞賜我們的善惡，賞賜我們的好與不好。佛教主要是在講究人的行為，主張自己決定自己的一切，就是「自由業力」。每一個人做了好事的因，自然會生出好的業果，所以業力是非常自由的，它沒有什麼特殊，沒有什麼權威，所謂自作自受，就是佛道。

What are the Buddhist Teachings

When we speak of the Buddhist teachings, we are referring to the body of teachings that embody the truth of Buddhism. What is the truth of Buddhism? In reference to this question, I offer the following four points.

1. The Buddhist teachings are about individual karma.

Buddhism differs from other religions in that it does not believe in the existence of a god who directs our lives. It does not espouse the idea that there is a god who rewards or punishes us for our good or bad deeds. Buddhism believes that our own actions control our own destiny; thus it speaks of self-directing karma. When we do something good, it is like planting a good seed. This good seed will, of course, yield a good effect. Thus, karma is essentially under our own control. There is nothing unique or authoritative about the workings of karma. We reap what we sow; this is essence of Buddhist teachings.

第二，緣起中道是佛道：

佛教講究世間的一切都不是單獨存在的，而是彼此相互關係，因緣和合而生起的。所以不只說生不只說滅，不僅僅說有說無，它完全是一個中道。體解緣起中道的本性，就是佛道。

2. The Buddhist teachings are about conditioned arising and the Middle Way.

Buddhism teaches us that nothing in this world can exist independent of external conditions; we all exist in a web of interrelated causes and conditions. Thus, Buddhism does not only speak of becoming nor does it only speak of ceasing. Buddhism does not only talk about existence nor does it only talk about non-existence. Buddhism emphasizes the Middle Way; the law of conditioned arising and the Middle Way are at the heart of the Buddhist teachings.

第三，民主平等是佛道：

現在我們講求民主，佛教的教理最民主，人和佛沒有大小的分別，佛是一個覺悟的人，人是還沒有覺悟的佛。人和佛在本性上都是平等的，所謂生佛平等、男女平等、智愚平等，一切眾生都是平等的，這種民主平等的思想就是佛道。

3. The Buddhist teachings are about democracy and equality.

While we have to work for democracy in politics and government, the basic principles of Buddhism are the most democratic of all. The Buddhist teachings tell us that there is no superiority or inferiority between the Buddha and human beings. The Buddha is an enlightened man, while we are Buddhas yet to be enlightened. Our nature is equal to the Buddha s nature. Thus, there is equality between sentient beings and the Buddha, between man and woman, and between the intelligent and the slow. In fact, all sentient beings are equal.

This basic tenet of democracy and equality is inherent in the Buddhist teachings.

第四，　無我超越是佛道：

　每一個人都執著自我，因為執著自我，就有你，就有他，就有世界，就有人我對待，就有是非得失。假如無我，超脫了我相、人相、眾生相、壽者相、超越了一切而無相，那麼世界大同，人我一如，就是真正的佛道了。

4. The Buddhist teachings are about transcending the notion of self.

We all cling to the notion of self. Because of this attachment, a differentiation between me, you, others, and even the whole world exists. The duality of self and others, right versus wrong, and gain versus loss also arise because of the attachment to self. If we can comprehend selflessness and transcend the notion of self, then we will transcend everything without attachment to any notions. In this state of mind, we will look at the world with equanimity and look at self and others without distinction. This is indeed the teaching of Buddhism.

所以說，什麼是佛教的眞理？就是：

第一，　自由業力是佛道。
第二，　緣起中道是佛道。
第三，　民主平等是佛道。
第四，　無我超越是佛道。

In summary, what are the Buddhist teachings? They are:

1. Individual karma.
2. Conditioned arising and the Middle Way.
3. Democracy and equality.
4. Transcending the notion of self.

如何學道修行

How to Practice and Cultivate
According to Buddhism

我們在世間上做人，總想要做一個成功的人，總希望事業順利、課業進步、人際關係和諧、家庭幸福美滿...，最好做什麼都能有所成就。學道修行也是一樣，總希望對佛法真理有所體悟，以祈能了生脫死，活得自在。我要如何學道修行，才能開悟證果呢？我有四點意見貢獻給大家：

We all would like to be successful in life. We wish for a good education, a prosperous career, friends, and a happy family life. In short, we want to be able to achieve what we set out to do. Religious cultivation is no different; we wish to understand the Dharma so that we can live a carefree life and be free of the cycle of birth and death. How do we practice and cultivate ourselves so we may attain enlightenment? I want to offer you the following four suggestions:

第一，從淡處著眼：

學道修行的人不要太執迷於感情而被感情束縛，不要什麼事都希望別人以濃情厚意待我，有時候感情太濃烈了反而不能長久。所謂「君子之交淡如水」，青菜蘿蔔雖然味淡，若是天天吃，青菜蘿蔔也會吃出滋味來的。

1. Appreciate simplicity.

In our efforts to practice the Dharma, we have to learn not to be attached or bound by our emotions. It is best for our practice if our relationships with others are level and smooth; intense relationships often do not last long. There is a Chinese saying, A gentlemanly relationship is as plain as water. Simple vegetables may taste bland, but if we eat them everyday, we will discover the unique taste of even the simplest greens.

第二，從無處下手：

　　無，不是沒有。無中可以生有，所謂「真空生妙有」，要先「空」才能「有」。比方說：一塊空地，什麼都沒有，才可以建高樓；心裏沒有成見，才能接受真理；茶杯要空，才能裝茶水，才有甘醇的茶水可以喝，假如茶杯裏面已經有了酒、油，味道就變質了。因此，無，並非不好，從「無」裏面可以體會更多。我們做事也要有從「無」開始的觀念，不要希望人家都為我做好、準備好，真正有用的人是能夠從空無的地方成就一切。

第三，從疑處用心：

　　佛教和其他宗教不同，它重視「疑」。所謂小疑小悟、大疑大悟、不疑不悟。要在學道上用心發掘問題，此即禪宗所謂的「參話頭」。能把一句話緊緊守住，行住坐臥都不離，在疑惑處下手，如此學道才有消息。

2. Start from nothingness.

Nothingness does not mean being without anything, because something can, indeed, arise from nothing. The saying, From true emptiness emerges many wondrous things, tells us that emptiness is the basis of existence. For example, take a vacant lot. It is because it has nothing on it that a building can be constructed there. Similarly, our minds have to be free of prejudice before we can accept the truth of the Dharma. The cup must be empty before it can hold tea or water for us to drink. If the cup already contains wine or oil, the tea would taste different. Thus, the state of nothingness is not necessarily bad; it can teach us many things. In our undertakings, we should start with the expectation of nothingness. Those who are truly capable do not expect others to do everything for them; they can achieve their goals even when starting from nothing.

3. Be doubtful.

Buddhism differs from other religions in that it emphasizes the importance of being doubtful. Doubts are the seeds of enlightenment, without which enlightenment would not be possible. We should always ask questions in the course of our practice. In the Chan school, there is a method of practice that requires a student to contemplate a saying. If the student is able to contemplate a certain saying at all times and keeps asking questions about it, the student will no doubt improve by deepening his or her understanding.

第四，從拙處力行：

抱著笨拙的心去學道，古人曾說：「勤能補拙」，我做任何事，只要能精勤力行，終有寸進。

4. Work diligently on our shortcomings.

If we are mindful of our shortcomings when we practice, we will definitely make progress. Just as the old saying goes, Diligence can compensate for many of our shortcomings, as long as we work hard in everything we do, we will be able to make steady progress.

要如何學道修行呢？就是：

第一，從淡處著眼。

第二，從無處下手。

第三，從疑處用心。

第四，從拙處力行。

How should we practice our cultivation? We should:

1. Appreciate simplicity.
2. Start from nothingness.
3. Be doubtful.
4. Work diligently on our shortcomings.

學佛的利益

The Benefits of Learning Buddhism

有人問，我們信仰宗教，究竟有什麼利益呢？學佛的利益是什麼？

People often ask, What are the benefits of having faith in a religion? What are the benefits of learning Buddhism? Buddhism can help us to:

第一， 認識真理，明瞭人生：

學佛的最大利益，就是認識宇宙人生的真理。比方說：這個世界是怎麼形成的？人生的真相是什麼？生從何處來？死往何處去？你對佛教有了認識，你就知道人的生死情況，知道世界的還滅。雖然，世界是成住壞空的，人生是生老病死的，但並非成住壞空、生老病死就什麼都沒有。成住壞空是循環的，生老病死也不是一死了之；壞空後仍有成住，死後還是會復生，所以五趣流轉、六道輪迴之間的種種情況，都值得我們去探討。

1. Know the truth and understand life.

The greatest benefit of learning Buddhism is learning the truth regarding life and the universe. For example, how was our world formed? What is the real picture of life? Where does life come from? Where do we go after death? The Buddhist teachings instruct us about life and death, and about the formation and cessation of the world. On one hand, we realize that the world goes through stages of formation, abiding, destruction and emptiness, and that life is a process of birth, aging, sickness, and death. On the other hand, we understand that these stages and processes do not negate the existence of everything. The stages of formation, abiding, destruction and emptiness are a cycle. After the stages of destruction and emptiness, there are the stages of formation and abiding. The life process of birth, aging, sickness, and death does not mean that life ends with death. There is rebirth after death. In fact, it is worth our while to study the subject of rebirth within the six realms of existence.

第二，走出自我，開拓胸懷：

如果沒有佛教的信仰，我們就會生活在自我中心裏，被虛妄的自我迷惑。因而我們執著，我們貪戀，跳不出自我，不能超越自我，在貪瞋痴的泥沼裏輾轉生活，是很不自在的。我們如果有佛學的素養，走出自我，開拓胸懷，視眾生都是我的兄弟姊妹，宇宙世間都是我的道場，那真是一個無限寬廣的人生。

2. Move away from self-centeredness and expand our horizons.

Without the benefits of the Buddhist teachings, we tend to live in a self-centered world. We become deluded by the concept of self and cannot let go. Because we cling to our attachments, we cannot transcend the self and are mired in a life of greed, hatred, and ignorance. With the Buddhist teachings, we can move away from self-centeredness and learn to expand our horizons. We can view all sentient beings as our siblings and see the entire universe as our place of enlightenment. This is indeed a broad and boundless life.

第三，培養人格，昇華擴大：

在宗教裏，最重視人格的完成，要把我們的自我昇華擴大，擴大到「心包太虛，量周沙界」，把我們的人格培養成道德圓滿的人生。

3. Nurture our character and elevate our minds.

Buddhism, like every religion, places a great deal of emphasis on character development. Buddhism also teaches us to elevate and expand our minds, just like the saying, The mind encompasses the space of the universe, traversing realms as numerous as the grains of sand in the Ganges River. With the benefits of the Buddhist teachings, we all can learn to nurture our character and live a complete and virtuous life.

第四，享受法樂，常行精進：

我們信奉佛教，最主要的是享受真理的快樂。世俗上的娛樂短暫易失，法樂裏的人生快樂卻深廣無限。

4. Enjoy the joys of the Dharma and practice with diligence.

Most importantly, Buddhism can help us to enjoy the joys of the truth. Worldly pleasures are transient and fade away easily. The joys of the Dharma can bring us a limitless and happy life.

所以學佛的利益有四種：

第一，認識真理，明瞭人生。

第二，走出自我，開拓胸懷。

第三，培養人格，昇華擴大。

第四，享受法樂，常行精進。

There are four benefits to learning Buddhism. Buddhism can help us to:

1. Know the truth and understand life.
2. Move away from self-centeredness and expand our horizons.
3. Nurture our character and elevate our minds.
4. Enjoy the joys of the Dharma and practice with diligence.

皈依的認識

近年來信仰佛教的風氣很盛，多少人來到佛門，皈依了三寶。皈依三寶是皈投依靠三寶的意思。皈依的真正意義是什麼呢？

In recent years, many people have turned to Buddhism, and we often hear of people taking refuge in the Triple Gem. Taking refuge is a ceremony in which we commit ourselves to the Triple Gem of the Buddha, the Dharma, and the Sangha. Here are some basic points we should understand about taking refuge.

第一，皈依不是吃素齋、不是受戒約束、不是剃度出家：

皈依是表示我信仰佛教，假如沒有經過皈依這個儀禮，只是拜拜、燒香，都不算佛教徒，只能算是一個佛教的尊敬者。做一個佛教徒，必須經過皈依的程序。

皈依不是吃素，與吃素沒有關係。不皈依的人也可以吃素，皈依的人也可以不吃素。

1. Taking refuge is different from practicing vegetarianism, upholding the precepts, and joining the Sangha.

Taking refuge in the Triple Gem is an expression of one s faith in Buddhism. Without going through the rite of taking refuge in the Triple Gem, one is not considered a Buddhist. We may show our respect to the Buddha by going to the temple and burning incense sticks, but to become a Buddhist, we need to take refuge in the Triple Gem. Taking refuge in the Triple Gem does not mean that one has to become a vegetarian. They are two different things. Many vegetarians have not taken refuge in the Triple Gem, and many who have taken refuge in the Triple Gem are not vegetarians.

皈依不是受戒，皈依沒有什麼
戒條約束，假如有，也是說我信
仰佛教，我不改變信心。與五
戒、菩薩戒都是不相干的。

因此，皈依不是吃素、不是受
戒，當然更不是出家。

第二，皈依不是皈依神、不是皈依師父、不是酬謝報償：

皈依之後，仍然可以拜神，例
如媽祖、城隍、關公、仙公等，
那是一種恭敬。我們對不同宗教
的人不是也握手、敬禮嗎？所以
神是可以拜的，但並非皈依。

皈依三寶時，主持皈依的法師
師父只是給我們做個證明的師
父，證明我們是三寶弟子、是佛
教徒。因此，皈依不是拜師父。

皈依不是為了要酬謝、感恩神
明，而是堅定自己的人生信仰，
所以不能隨便。

Many people also confuse taking refuge with taking the precepts. Taking refuge is different from taking the Five Precepts or the Bodhisattva Precepts. In fact, when we take refuge, the only observance we have to keep is our commitment and devotion to Buddhism. Last but not least, taking refuge does not mean that we have to renounce the household life to join the Sangha.

2. Taking refuge does not preclude us from showing respect to gods of other belief systems; it is not a pledge of allegiance to an individual master; and it is not an expression of gratitude.

After we have taken refuge in the Triple Gem, we can still show our respect to gods of other belief systems. When we meet someone of another faith, we still show our courtesy and extend our help. Likewise, we can still show our respect to gods of other religions, for a show of respect is very different from the commitment of taking refuge. Taking refuge is an expression of a devotee s pledge to the Triple Gem of the Buddha, the Dharma, and the Sangha. The ceremonial master is a witness to the devotees pledge, and we should not be mistaken into thinking that when we take refuge, we are pledging our allegiance to an individual master. Taking refuge is a symbol to show our commitment; it is definitely not a means to thank the divine for their help and blessings. As such, we should not take refuge lightly.

第三，皈依不是一時的、不是只一次的、不是一皈依的：

不能說只皈依佛，就不皈依法，不皈依僧；皈依是皈依三寶，是佛、法、僧一體皈依。皈依更是終生的信仰，一生以佛陀的教法為依歸，做一個健全的佛弟子。

3. Taking refuge is not a limited-scope or short-term commitment.

When we take refuge in the Triple Gem, we take refuge in the Buddha, the Dharma, and the Sangha. We cannot selectively take refuge in one and not the others. Taking refuge is a lifelong commitment. When we take refuge, we are essentially saying that we will seek refuge in the Buddha s teachings and that we will forever be true followers of the Buddha.

因此，我們對於皈依的認識，應該是：

第一，皈依不是吃素齋、不是受戒約束、不是剃度出家。

第二，皈依不是皈依神、不是皈依師父、不是酬謝報償。

第三，皈依不是一時的、不是只一次的、不是一皈依的。

What do we understand about taking refuge?

1. Taking refuge is different from practicing vegetarianism, upholding the precepts, and joining the Sangha.

2. Taking refuge does not preclude us from showing respect to gods of other belief systems; it is not a pledge of allegiance to an individual master; and it is not an expression of gratitude.

3. Taking refuge is not a limited-scope or short-term commitment.

受戒的好處

目前社會上，有一個很好的現象，就是每年都有幾十萬人，在全國各地寺院受戒：受五戒、菩薩戒。為什麼這麼多人要去受佛教的戒律呢？這是現代提倡法治社會的必然現象，因為在法治的社會中，大家都要守法，在佛教的信徒就是要受戒。

受戒有什麼好處呢？我有六點意見：

第一，戒如良師：

戒，就像我們的老師一樣，什麼能做，什麼不能做，它指示我們方向。

Why Should We Observe the Precepts

In modern day Taiwan, a wonderful trend is in the making. Every year, several hundreds of thousands of people take the precepts in temples all over Taiwan. Some people observe the Five Precepts; others observe the Bodhisattva Precepts. Why do all these people want to observe these precepts? Actually, this is a very natural phenomenon. In the law-abiding society of today, everyone is expected to follow the law; likewise, in Buddhism, Buddhists also choose to observe the various precepts of our religion.

There are many reasons why we should observe the precepts. I offer the following six reasons as food for thought.

1. Precepts are like teachers.

Precepts function like a good teacher; they let us know what we should and should not do. They point us in the direction of all good qualities.

第二，戒如軌道：

可以規範我們的行為。比方說：佛法，可以規範我們的進退，可以引導我們的行事。

第三，戒如城池：

可以防護外人的侵犯。一個守戒的人，平常不亂殺生，不亂偷盜，也不亂淫，不亂說，不亂吃，不作一切非法的事情，所謂「平常不作虧心事，夜半敲門心不驚」，所以戒如城池。

第四，戒如水囊：

可以解除人生旅途上的乾涸。戒告訴我們：這個不可以，那個不可以，讓我們不生起貪欲心、瞋恨心，不會為非作歹，如同得到甘露灌頂，時時清涼自在。

2. Precepts are like railroad tracks.

Tracks keep trains on course; likewise, precepts help us to stay on course. Precepts can shape our sense of propriety and guide our actions.

3. Precepts are like moats.

Like a moat that safeguards a castle, precepts help us fend off temptations. When we uphold the precepts, we abstain from killing, stealing, sexual misconduct, idle speech, and intoxicants. When we are mindful of our actions, we feel secure and peaceful. This is reflected in the saying, If we do not do anything to compromise our integrity, we will not be afraid when [judgment] comes knocking on our door.

4. Precepts are like water canteens.

Like a water canteen that can relieve the thirst of a traveler, precepts quench the thirst of desire on the journey of life. Precepts gently remind us of that from which we should abstain. They teach us not to let greed, hatred, and ill thoughts arise in our minds. Precepts are like sweet dew, which helps us stay cool and peaceful at all times.

第五，戒如明燈：

可以照亮前程的黑暗。我們一受戒，戒條明明白白告誡我們：不可以侵犯人，不可以罵人，不可以打人，不可以作壞事，等於人生前程的一盞明燈，讓我們看清楚前途何去何從，不至於走岔了路，不至於摸黑傾跌。

第六，戒如瓔珞：

可以莊嚴我們的法身。每個人都希望穿著高雅，都希望有美麗的妝扮。戒就是瓔珞，就好像穿在我們身上的美麗的衣服，可以莊嚴我們的相貌。一個受戒的人，就有道德人格來莊嚴自己。

受戒的好處，就有六種：

第一，戒如良師。
第二，戒如軌道。
第三，戒如城池。
第四，戒如水囊。
第五，戒如明燈。
第六，戒如瓔珞。

5. Precepts are like bright lights.

Precepts can help us see where we are heading, just like a bright light that helps a traveler see the road. When we observe the precepts, we learn not to violate the rights of others. They shine for us like a bright light so that we will not walk astray and fall into darkness.

6. Precepts are like gems.

Precepts can beautify our spiritual being. Some people like to wear fine jewelry so that they look elegant and charming. Precepts are like gems, they help us beautify our appearance. A person who observes the precepts adorns himself or herself with virtuous action.

Precepts act in many different capacities and help us to enrich our lives, as follows:

1. Precepts are like teachers.
2. Precepts are like railroad tracks.
3. Precepts are like moats.
4. Precepts are like water canteens.
5. Precepts are like bright lights.
6. Precepts are like gems.

涅槃是不生不滅，
沒有生死，超越時間和空間，
泯除人我的對待，不在生死中流轉。

*...Nirvana is liberation from birth and death, time and space,
and dualities such as self versus other. Nirvana is a state
where there is no birth or death; it is a perfect and everlasting
state...*

何謂佛性

何謂佛性？佛性就是成佛的性能。每一個人都有成佛的性能，只是自己不知道罷了。當初釋迦牟尼佛在印度菩提樹下金剛座上開悟，悟道以後，第一句話就說：『奇哉！奇哉！大地眾生皆有如來智慧德相，只因妄想執著而不能得。』

什麼是如來的佛性呢？就是每一個人本來具有的性能。任何東西都有性能，性能好價值就高；人也有性能，比方說我能苦能樂、能忙能閒、能早能晚、能飽能餓，這表示性能很好。因此每個人都要發揮自己的性能，甚至於將來都可以成聖成賢、成佛做祖。

What is Buddha Nature

Where is Buddha Nature? Buddha Nature is something we all have; it is our ability to become Buddhas. We all have the potential to become a Buddha, yet we are blind to this capability that is latent in all of us. When Sakyamuni Buddha became enlightened under the bodhi tree, his first word was, Surprise! All living beings have the wisdom and qualities of a Tathagata, but our delusions and attachments have hindered our ability to realize this wisdom.

What is Buddha Nature? Basically, it is something inherent within each of us. Everything has its attributes. Good attributes are of good value. We are no different; we all have our attributes. For instance, if I am an adaptable person, then I can take the good and the bad. I can keep a busy schedule and yet be content with nothing to do. I can get up early in the morning or stay up late into the night. I can eat a lot or fast for a few days. These are flexible qualities. We all should develop our inherent qualities and live up to our potential so that one day we may become a sage, a virtuous person, or a Buddha.

何謂佛性呢？

第一，處凡愚而不減：

雖為凡夫，處在愚痴的人生裏，佛性並沒有減少，而且是人人本具、個個不減的。

第二，在聖賢而不增：

對佛、菩薩而言，佛性是不增不減的，所以說心、佛、眾生，三無差別。佛是已覺悟的人，而人是沒有覺悟的佛。覺悟有先後，但佛性是平等的。

第三，住煩惱而不亂：

人在煩惱裏，儘管有是非人我，佛性卻絲毫不亂。就好像黃金，你把它做成金戒子、金耳環、金手鐲，甚至於金筷子、金碗、金手錶，雖然千差萬別，可

The following are some of the characteristics of Buddha Nature.

1. Buddha Nature does not decrease.

Though we live in the saha world as unenlightened individuals, our Buddha Nature is not compromised. We all have Buddha Nature, not lessened in any degree.

2. Buddha Nature does not increase.

The sage and the virtuous do not have any greater claim on Buddha Nature than any one of us. All Buddhas and bodhisattvas have the same Buddha Nature that we all have. Thus, we say that our mind, all Buddhas, and all beings are essentially the same. A Buddha is an enlightened individual, and sentient beings are Buddhas yet to be enlightened. Each one of us may realize enlightenment at a different pace, but our Buddha Nature is always the same.

3. Buddha Nature is forever constant.

In our daily lives, we often become distracted by worries and troubles. Our delusions cannot corrupt our Buddha Nature. Take the example of gold. We can mold a piece of gold into a gold ring, a pair

是黃金的本性是不變、不亂的。
所以我們人儘管在五趣六道裏面
流轉，驢腹馬胎，佛性仍不亂不
變的。

of gold earrings, a gold bracelet, a gold watch, or even a gold bowl. Though it may take on many different forms, its original nature is essentially unchanged. As we go through our many cycles of rebirth, our Buddha Nature remains unchanged.

第四，居禪定而不寂：

在禪定裏，佛性是朗朗光照，
如明鏡能照見萬物，不失功能。

4. Buddha Nature is like a mirror.

Even in meditative concentration, our Buddha Nature shines clearly, like a mirror, reflecting everything in this world.

每一個人本自具足的佛性是什麼？

第一，處凡愚而不減。
第二，在聖賢而不增。
第三，住煩惱而不亂。
第四，居禪定而不寂。

Thus, what are the characteristics of Buddha Nature? They are:

1. Buddha Nature does not decrease.
2. Buddha Nature does not increase.
3. Buddha Nature is forever constant.
4. Buddha Nature is like a mirror.

佛教的特性

時常有人問我：佛教的特性是什麼？我認為佛教有六大特性：

People often ask me, What are the characteristics of Buddhism? I believe Buddhism has six main characteristics.

第一，與眾生相應的人間性：

佛教是為眾生而設，為人類需要而設的宗教，所以它有人間性。人類需要有道德的規範，佛教就講道德情操；人類需要人格的昇華，佛教就重視人格昇華；人類重視了生脫死、滅除煩惱，佛教就有許多生死解脫的方便法門。

1. Buddhism is humanistic and addresses the needs of all sentient beings.

Buddhism is a religion for all sentient beings, and it addresses the needs of the human race. People need moral guidelines; Buddhism teaches us about morality. People need integrity; Buddhism emphasizes integrity. People want liberation from birth and death, and they want relief from their troubles and problems; Buddhism provides many Dharma methods to teach us how to free ourselves from the cycle of birth and death.

第二，與眾生和合的生活性：

眾生在世間誰也離不開生活。人間生活最要緊的就是：生活要和諧，生活要和合，因為世間不是一個人的，是大家共同相依生活的，所以佛教與眾生有和合的生活性。

2. Buddhism is about peace and harmony in everyday living.

As long as we are in this world, we have to be concerned with everyday living. The most important aspects of everyday living are harmony and unity. The world does not belong to a single individual. It is a place where life depends on interconnection. Buddhism is about peace and harmony in everyday living.

第三，與眾生有利的慈悲性：

我們活在世間上，佛教對我們最大的利益，就是指導我們如何慈悲，如何實踐慈悲，佛教最具有這個慈悲性。

第四，與眾生快樂的喜悅性：

佛教是幸福的宗教，是快樂的宗教，是喜悅的宗教。有時候佛教所以講煩惱，講痛苦，就是要你知解之後離開煩惱，離開痛苦，才能快樂，才能喜悅。

第五，與眾生肯定的平等性：

我們的社會，大家都講自由，都講民主，自由民主是建築在平等的上面。所以釋迦牟尼佛成道的時候，就發表一個宣言：「大地眾生皆有如來智慧德相。」一切眾生皆有佛性，所以大家都是平等的，心、佛、眾生三無差別。佛教給予眾生肯定的平等性。

3. Buddhism teaches us compassion.

The greatest benefit that Buddhism has bestowed upon us is that it teaches us how to be compassionate and how to act compassionately. Compassion is the most prominent characteristic of Buddhism.

4. Buddhism is joyous and brings happiness to all sentient beings.

Buddhism is a religion of happiness and joy. The reason that Buddhism teaches us about worry and suffering is to help us have a better understanding of them. Only then can we learn to free ourselves of worries and attain joy and happiness.

5. Buddhism affirms equality for all sentient beings.

In our society, we like to talk about liberty and democracy. Liberty and democracy are built upon equality. When Sakyamuni Buddha gained enlightenment, he pronounced, All sentient beings on earth possess wisdom and Buddha Nature. Since we all have Buddha Nature, everyone is equal. Our mind, the Buddha, and all sentient beings are not different from one another. Buddhism affirms equality for all sentient beings.

第六，與眾生認同的普濟性：

佛教具有普濟社會大眾的性格，大家相攜相扶，相讓相助，才能共同解脫，共同自在。

佛教的特性是什麼？就是：

第一，與眾生相應的人間性。

第二，與眾生和合的生活性。

第三，與眾生有利的慈悲性。

第四，與眾生快樂的喜悅性。

第五，與眾生肯定的平等性。

第六，與眾生認同的普濟性。

6. Buddhism teaches us to lend a helping hand to others.

Buddhism teaches us to have care and concern for our fellow men and women. When we help each other, we can all be at ease and attain liberation.

What are the characteristics of Buddhism? They are:

1. Buddhism is humanistic and addresses the needs of all sentient beings.
2. Buddhism is about peace and harmony in everyday living.
3. Buddhism teaches us compassion.
4. Buddhism is joyous and brings happiness to all sentient beings.
5. Buddhism affirms equality for all sentient beings.
6. Buddhism teaches us to lend a helping hand to others.

大乘佛教的精神

佛教有大乘、小乘之分。有人問,什麼是大乘佛教?什麼又是小乘佛教?簡單的說,小乘是自度,大乘是度人的。「乘」是車乘,小乘是小的車子,可以載一個人,所以叫小乘;大乘是大車子,可以載很多人,所以叫大乘。大家應該學習大乘佛教,大乘的精神有六點:

第一,以布施來度人:

度人首重布施,布施給人利益,給人快樂,給人歡喜,給人方便。

第二,以持戒來節欲:

人的欲望是無窮無盡的,節制欲望要靠持戒。持戒就是約束不當的、不好的,凡不可為的皆不能做。

The Spirit of Mahayana Buddhism

There are two main branches of Buddhism, namely, Mahayana and Hinayana. Someone may ask: What is the difference between Mahayana Buddhism and Hinayana Buddhism? Simply speaking, Hinayana Buddhism focuses on self-liberation, while Mahayana Buddhism focuses on the liberation of others. Yana is a Sanskrit term for vehicle. Hinayana, meaning lesser vehicle, has been used as a derogatory term by some Mahayanists. Mahayana means great vehicle, which can hold many individuals. There are six basic principles in Mahayana Buddhism:

1. Deliver others by giving to others.

To deliver others, we have to first practice generosity. Generosity can help others, bring happiness to others, and bring convenience to others.

2. Control our desires by observing the precepts.

Given that our desires are endless and boundless, it is very important for us to control our desires through the observance of precepts. Upholding the precepts can help us refrain from inappropriate, unwholesome, and unbecoming behavior.

第三，以忍辱來修持：

最大的修養就是忍辱。佛陀經常教誡我們，布施持戒功德都不及忍辱。「忍一口氣，風平浪靜」，忍的功德很大，可以消災免難。

3. Cultivate patience and tolerance.

One of the highest forms of cultivation is tolerance, especially in the face of hostility. The Buddha always teaches us to be tolerant. In fact, the merits of tolerance surpass that of giving to others and observing the precepts. There is a Chinese proverb that aptly describes the power of tolerance, A little tolerance can quiet the wind and calm the sea. The merit gained from being tolerant is great and can divert misfortune and calamity.

第四，以精進來降魔：

社會上有聲色、名利的魔；內心裏有貪瞋、煩惱、七情六欲的魔。如果要降魔，必須要有精進的精神、勇氣、毅力。學佛修行和作戰一樣，要用精進勇猛和煩惱的魔王作戰。

4. Quell temptations through right effort.

Externally, we have to deal with the temptations of fame and fortune; internally, we have to deal with the hindrances of greed, hatred, worries, the seven emotions (pleasure, anger, sorrow, joy, love, hate, and desire), and the six forms of attraction (color, form, mannerism, voice, softness, and features). If we are to arrest these temptations, we have to develop the right spirit, courage, and endurance. In a way, practicing our cultivation is not unlike going into battle. We have to arm ourselves with courage and perseverance to fend off these temptations.

第五，以禪定來安住：

我們安住在金錢裏，金錢被人倒閉就煩惱；安住在愛情裏，當愛情起變化就煩惱；安住在朋友間，朋友離開了也要煩惱；最好安住在禪定裏，處變不驚，以不變應萬變。

5. Anchor ourselves in meditative concentration.

If we anchor our identity in wealth, we may lose our minds when our money is lost. If we anchor our identity in love, we will worry when there is uncertainty in our relationships. If we anchor our identity in friends, afflictions can arise when our friends leave us. Thus, it is best for us to anchor ourselves in meditative concentration. In this way, we will not be swayed or feel threatened by external circumstances; we can confront the changing world with unchanging fortitude.

第六，以般若來化惡：

以般若智慧化除世間上的種種惡事、惡因緣，才能自度度人。

6. Transform depravity through prajna wisdom.

We have to use prajna to transform the evil deeds and evil causes and conditions of this world. Only then can we deliver ourselves as well as others.

因此，大乘佛教的精神是：

第一，以布施來度人。

第二，以持戒來節欲。

第三，以忍辱來修持。

第四，以精進來降魔。

第五，以禪定來安住。

第六，以般若來化惡。

The spirit of Mahayana is summed up in the following six points:

1. Deliver others by giving to others.
2. Control our desires by observing the precepts.
3. Cultivate patience and tolerance.
4. Quell temptations through right effort.
5. Anchor ourselves in meditative concentration.
6. Transform depravity through prajna wisdom.

禪門的生活

禪，不是佛教的專有品；禪，是我們每一個人所有的，是我們每一個人的心，是我們每一個人的生活；禪，是我們每一個人應該認識，應該擁有的修養。禪門的生活是：

第一，從忍辱中去除無明：

禪是一種力量，是所謂「定力」。你有定力才能忍辱，才能從忍辱裏去除一些怨恨、瞋恚、無明、煩惱，才能獲得安定生活。

第二，從作務中培養福報：

禪，不是兀兀呆坐；禪，是活潑潑的作務。比方說：百丈禪師的「一日不作，一日不食」，而歷代的禪師也都是從作務中去培養人緣，培養福報，培養功德。

第三，從修福中增長智慧：

一個禪者，對社會不但盡心公益、慈善，他從慈善公益的事業

The Life of Chan Practice

Chan is not a specialty of Buddhism; it is something we all have. Chan is the mind and life of each of us. Chan is a practice each of us should learn. The life of Chan practice is:

1. To eradicate ignorance through tolerance.

Chan is a kind of power, what we call samadhi (power of concentration). If we have this power, then we will be tolerant. With tolerance, we will eradicate grudges, anger, ignorance, and worries in life. Thus, we will achieve peace and harmony in living.

2. To cultivate merits through work.

Chan is not immobile sitting. Chan is actually lively work. Chan Master Baizhang practiced, No work for the day, no meals for the day. Chan masters throughout history cultivated affinities and merits through work.

3. To perfect wisdom by cultivating merits.

A Chan practitioner works hard to perform charity work for others.

裏面知道迴向，還知道無相，還知道擴大胸襟，這叫做智慧。禪，就是福慧雙修。

He or she also knows that in the process, he or she should transfer the merits, expand his or her mind, and not develop attachments. This is called wisdom. Chan is the practice of cultivating both merits and wisdom.

第四，從感恩中獲得快樂：

我們常常要歡喜，要快樂，歡喜快樂不一定從貪欲中獲得。有時候從喜捨裏面獲得歡喜，從感恩裏面獲得快樂。禪者有一種感恩的心理，對天地的感恩，對三寶的感恩，對師友、父母的感恩，對社會、國家的感恩，他從感恩裏面覺得滿足，覺得快樂。

4. To achieve happiness through gratitude.

We all want to be happy and filled with joy. Happiness and joy do not come exclusively from satisfying personal desire. Sometimes happiness can be gained from a feeling of gratitude. A Chan practitioner is always grateful towards heaven and earth; towards the Triple Gem; towards parents, friends, and teachers; and towards society and country. He or she can achieve satisfaction and happiness from gratitude.

第五，從參禪中解脫自在：

從平常參禪的修養裏，他就能昇華，就能擴大，就能淨化，就能解脫，就能獲得自由自在。

5. To attain liberation and freedom.

Through the practice of Chan, a practitioner can achieve sublimation, expansion, and purification. Then, he or she can become liberated and attain freedom.

所以禪門的生活有五：

第一，從忍辱中去除無明。

第二，從作務中培養福報。

第三，從修福中增長智慧。

第四，從感恩中獲得快樂。

第五，從參禪中解脫自在。

Therefore, the five aspects in the life of Chan practice are:

1. To eradicate ignorance through tolerance.
2. To cultivate merits through work.
3. To perfect wisdom by cultivating merits.
4. To achieve happiness through gratitude.
5. To attain liberation and freedom.

涅槃是什麼

What is the Meaning of Nirvana

涅槃這兩個字，很深奧，一般人不容易了解，以為涅槃就是死亡的意思，這是錯誤的。涅槃就是人不死亡，才叫做涅槃。涅槃是不生不滅，沒有生死，超越時間和空間，泯除人我的對待，不在生死中流轉。涅槃，是一種不生不死的境界，是圓滿、永恆的生命。我們每天修行、精進，就是為了證悟涅槃。當初釋迦牟尼佛在菩提樹下金剛座上成道，就是證悟涅槃的境界 —— 不生不死的境界。涅槃的真正意義是：

The meaning of the word nirvana is very deep and profound. Most people misunderstand its meaning. Some people think that nirvana means death. This is incorrect, for the word nirvana means deathless. Nirvana is liberation from birth and death, time and space, and dualities such as self versus the other. Nirvana is a state where there is no birth or death; it is a perfect and everlasting state. When the Buddha became enlightened under the bodhi tree, he entered a realm without the cycle of birth and death. The Buddha realized the true meaning of nirvana. We practice the Buddha s teachings so that we, too, may one day realize nirvana. So, what is the meaning of nirvana?

第一，是佛教追求本源的真理：

涅槃是個真理，是我們的本源，是我們的真心，是諸佛如來的佛性。

1. Nirvana is the state of truth.

Nirvana is the truth and our original self-nature. Nirvana is our pure mind and Buddha Nature.

第二，是人類探究永恆的價值：

我們都希望生命不只是幾十寒暑，而是永恆的。色身有生老病

2. Nirvana is everlasting.

All of us wish we could live forever and not just for a few decades. Unfortunately, our physical

116

死，可是我們的真心、我們的本性卻是永恒的，沒有生死的。涅槃，能讓我們探究永恒的價值。

bodies have a limited life span. Though our bodies have to go through birth, old age, sickness, and death, our Buddha Nature is ever-lasting. When we understand the true meaning of nirvana, we can experience eternity.

第三，是快樂幸福的終極歸宿：
我們所嚮往的快樂、幸福，與世俗的快樂、幸福是相對的；世俗的幸福是染污性、短暫性、變易性，是不究竟的，涅槃就是清淨的快樂、幸福，是我們圓滿的歸宿。

3. Nirvana is joy and happiness.
Worldly happiness is often short-lived and incomplete. In some cases, our happiness is accompanied by the agony of others. In contrast, the happiness of nirvana is pure, tranquil, and fulfilling.

第四，是常樂我淨的美滿境界：
涅槃是真常、真樂、真我、真淨的圓滿人生。

4. Nirvana is pure and complete.
Nirvana is the realm of permanence, joy, and purity. In nirvana, our Buddha Nature shines completely.

所以涅槃的意義就是：
第一，是佛教追求本源的真理。
第二，是人類探究永恒的價值。
第三，是快樂幸福的終極歸宿。
第四，是常樂我淨的美滿境界。

Thus, we can use the following to describe nirvana:
1. Nirvana is the state of truth.
2. Nirvana is everlasting.
3. Nirvana is joy and happiness.
4. Nirvana is pure and complete.

極樂淨土

一般人信仰佛教，除了希望現世生活幸福、美滿外，更希望將來能往生西方極樂世界。極樂世界到底有什麼好處，值得我們去往生呢？它有六個特色：

第一，沒有經濟的困擾：

在極樂世界裏，思衣得衣，思食得食，一切所需，隨念即得，由於沒有金錢的交易，因此沒有經濟的困擾。

第二，沒有男女的糾紛：

世間上，因為有男女，就時常有情愛的糾紛、苦惱；而在西方極樂世界，所有的人都是蓮花化生，沒有男女的分別，所以沒有情愛的糾紛。

The World of Ultimate Bliss

Many buddhists look to Buddhism not only for ways to live a happy and satisfying life in this lifetime, they also hope to be reborn in the Western Pure Land of Ultimate Bliss. Why do people want to be reborn in the Western Pure Land of Ultimate Bliss? Why is this Pure Land worthy of our pursuit? The Pure Land is unique in six ways:

1. There are no financial worries.

In the Pure Land, anyone who needs clothing will be clothed; anyone who needs food will be fed. The same is true of other necessities. The Pure Land is a place where money does not play a role. There are no financial worries and everyone is naturally well-provided for.

2. There are no gender-related problems.

Due to the existence of gender differences in our world, we often experience disagreements between men and women and, in particular, love-related problems. In the Western Pure Land of Ultimate Bliss, one is reborn there through the transformation of a lotus flower and there are no differences between genders. Thus, love-related problems do not exist in the Pure Land.

第三，沒有環境的污染：

極樂淨土有所謂的「黃金舖地、七重欄楯、七重樓閣、八功德水、微風吹動」等殊勝，可以說，在極樂世界裏，有最富麗堂皇的建築，有清新幽美的景緻，完全沒有環境的污染。

第四，沒有壞人的侵犯：

在極樂世界裏，沒有地獄、餓鬼、畜生等三惡道，只有「諸上善人，聚會一處」，所以沒有壞人的侵犯。

第五，沒有交通的事故：

極樂世界的人都是飛行自在，因此不會發生交通事故。

第六，沒有惡事的恐怖：

極樂淨土沒有惡人惡事，沒有

3. There is no environmental pollution.

In the sutras, we read that in the Pure Land the ground is covered with gold; there are seven rows of railings, seven layers of nets, and palaces seven stories high. The water has eight excellent qualities, and there is a constant gentle breeze blowing. The construction is remarkable; it is much more grand than any palace or building known to mankind. The environment is very pleasing, clean, and pristine. The exquisite architecture and the tranquil scenery indicate a land of purity, which is free of all environmental pollution.

4. There are no corrupt people.

The hell, ghost, and animal realms do not exist in the Pure Land. The Pure Land is a place of the good and the virtuous. There, we do not have to be fearful of scoundrels and villains.

5. There are no traffic problems.

In the Pure Land, everyone is at ease and able to fly to wherever he or she needs to go. There are no traffic problems in the Pure Land.

6. There is no terror of any kind.

As we have said earlier, the Pure Land is a place for the whole-

顛倒、恐怖、掛念、擔心等，所以人們在「無惡事恐怖」的環境裏，自由自在的生活。

假如我們生存的這個娑婆世界，人人都能遵禮守法，必能像極樂世界一樣，沒有金錢上、福利上、情愛上的糾紛，沒有環境的污染，沒有壞人的侵犯，沒有交通事故等惡事，那我們這個世界當下也就是極樂淨土了！

極樂淨土的六項特色是：

第一， 沒有經濟的困擾。

第二， 沒有男女的糾紛。

第三， 沒有環境的污染。

第四， 沒有壞人的侵犯。

第五， 沒有交通的事故。

第六， 沒有惡事的恐怖。

some and virtuous; thus, life in the Pure Land is pleasant and free of terror. Those who are reborn in the Pure Land are able to enjoy a land that is free, peaceful, and safe.

If all of us in this saha world were able to respect one other and abide by the law, then our world would be no different from the Pure Land. Then, we could live in a world free of economic struggles, emotional stress, environmental pollution, traffic chaos, and human-inflicted terror. As such, our world is also a Pure Land.

In summary, the six charac-teristics of the Pure Land are:

1. There are no financial worries.
2. There are no gender-related problems.
3. There is no environmental pol-lution.
4. There are no corrupt people.
5. There are no traffic problems.
6. There is no terror of any kind.

English Publication by
Venerable Master Hsing Yun

Buddha's Light Publishing:

1. Between Ignorance and Enlightenment (I)
2. Between Ignorance and Enlightenment(II)
3. The Awakening Life
4. Fo Guang Study
5. Sutra of the Medicine Buddha
   - with an Introduction, Comments and Prayer
6. From the Four Noble Truths to the Four Universal Vows
   - An Integration of the Mahayana and Theravada Schools
7. On Buddhist Democracy, Freedom and Equality
8. Of Benefit to Oneself and Others
   - A Critique of the Six Perfections

Wisdom Publications:

9. Only a Great Rain
   - A Guide to Chinese Buddhist Meditation
10. Describing the Indescribable
    - A Commentary on the Diamond Sutra

Weatherhill, Inc.:

11. Being Good
    - Buddhist Ethics for Everday Life
12. Lotus in a Stream
    - Basic Buddhism for Beginners

iUniverse.com, Inc.:

13. Humble Table, Wise Fare
    - Gift for Life

Peter Lang Publishing:

14. The Lion's Roar

Hsi Lai University Press:

Fogung Cultural Enterprise Co., Ltd.